BOLLINGEN SERIES XLV

The Collected Works of Paul Valéry

Edited by Jackson Mathews

VOLUME 2

PAUL VALÉRY

POEMS IN THE ROUGH

Translated by
Hilary Corke

With an Introduction by
Octave Nadal

BOLLINGEN SERIES XLV · 2

PRINCETON UNIVERSITY PRESS

PO
2643
A26
A23
Vol. 2

Burger

3/6/

THIS IS VOLUME TWO OF THE
COLLECTED WORKS OF PAUL VALÉRY
CONSTITUTING NUMBER XLV IN BOLLINGEN SERIES
SPONSORED BY BOLLINGEN FOUNDATION.
IT IS THE NINTH VOLUME OF THE
COLLECTED WORKS TO APPEAR

SBN   691—09845— ×

Library of Congress catalogue card no. 56–9337
Type composed at the University Printing House, Cambridge, England
Printed in the United States of America

DESIGNED BY ANDOR BRAUN

CONTENTS

INTRODUCTION, *by Octave Nadal*   xi

Parables   3

In Praise of Water   8

The Anagogical Revelation   12

The Angel   14

MIXTURE

Mixture Is Mind, 18 · *Sea,* 19 · *The Cathedral,* 20 · *At Grasse,*
21 · *Montpellier,* 23 · *Geneva,* 24 · *Tiger,* 24 · *The Same,* 25
Autumn, 26 · *Childhood Among Swans,* 26 · *Diamonds,* 27
Intelligence, 28 · *Hush!,* 29 · *The Empty and the Filled,* 30
Awaking, 30 · *Sketch,* 31 · *Aphorism,* 31 · *Mottoes,* 32 · *A
Haunted Room,* 32 · *Interior,* 33 · *Magic,* 34 · *A Dream,* 34 · *The
Poet's Shop,* 35 · *Seascape,* 35 · *"The Thinker,"* 36 · *Eye,* 36
Moments, 37 · *A Lady's Face,* 39 · *Seascape,* 39 · *Ideas,* 40 · *Gods,*
40 · *At Jehoshaphat,* 41 · *Amor,* 41 · *The Oyster,* 44 · *Psalm Y,* 45
Psalm Z, 46 · *A Matter of Employment,* 46 · *Pathos,* 47 · *Psycho-
Body Politic,* 48 · *Mouth,* 50 · *Alone,* 50 · *The Visionary,* 51
Singularities, 52 · *Psalm S,* 54 · *Birds,* 54 · *Waking,* 55 · *Psalm
T,* 56 · *Tears,* 56

POEMS IN THE ROUGH

Meditation Before Thought, 61 · *Motifs or Moments*, 63 · *In the Sun*, 65 · *To Life*, 65 · *At the End*, 66 · *Fifty Years Ago*, 66 *Dawn*, 66 · *Psalm Before the Beast*, 68 · *Song of the Master Notion*, 69

MOMENTS

The Test, 75 · *Of Colors*, 76 · *Mythology*, 77 · *The Universe*, 78 · *A Charitable Attention*, 78 · *In the Beginning Was the Fable*, 79 · *The Astonished Angel*, 79 · *Epigram*, 80 · *Animalities*, 80

BROKEN STORIES

Preface	87
Calypso	89
Crusoe	92
The Story of Hera	102
The Slave	105
Elisabeth to Rachel	110
Rachel	112
The Island of Xiphos	118
Acem	135
Poem	147
Fragments	148

CONTENTS

ODDS AND ENDS

London Bridge   155

Sketch   158

Dreams   159

Lost Verses   165

Seas   174

Psalm on a Voice   185

In the Square   187

The Old Woman   189

MINIATURES

The Young Mother, 193 · *The Flying Man*, 194 · *The Huntress*, 195 · *At the Races*, 195 · *Dance*, 196 · *Amazon*, 197 · *The Piano and the Song*, 198 · *Finery*, 199 · *The Holdup*, 199 · *Junk*, 200 *An Interior*, 201 · *The Screen*, 202

EARLY PIECES

Agatha   205

Pure Dramas   213

The Old Alleys   216

Unpublished Pages   218

VARIETY

ABC	223
Waiting	229
Midday	231
The Bath	233
Laura	235
The Unique	237
Greeting the Day	239
The Return	241
Psalm I	243
You Forget	244
Psalm II	245
Two Poems	246
Idea for a Story	247
Short Story	248
Work	249
Regarding the Sea	250
How to Make a Port	259
Power of Perfumes	262
Paris Is Here	265

CONTENTS

APPENDIX: From the Notebooks   273

NOTES   307

Introduction

FOR A LONG TIME nothing about Valéry seemed to me
more obvious than his predilection and his genius for the
verse poem. To my mind, the intensity, the purity, the
uniqueness of *La Jeune Parque, Le Cimetière marin, Le Serpent,*
made this entirely clear. Rightly or not, it was in these poems
that I found him most "changed into himself," for I have
always thought of the invention of form as the essence of the
creative act. The sign, too, of its authenticity, and in fact I
know of no other. To me it is wholly apparent that every
truly original stance of the mind, if it is to find expression,
must have at its command a new language corresponding in
form to the mystery that inhabits it, a language having a
pace, a manner, a quality—a shape, as it were, or presence
unlike any other. Which means that it must be created. Is it
not remarkable, for example, that the phrase *Que sais-je?*, so
perfectly expressing suspension of judgment and a particular
intellectual temper, led Montaigne to discover the *essay*,
which with the dialogue is still the literary form best adapted
to the skeptical attitude? The *thoughts* of Pascal, those dark
uninhabited meteors, bear inscribed in their riven structure
the contours of an anguish that cannot be composed. Lamar-
tine must be acknowledged as the creator of the *lyric of
meditation*; Rimbaud, of the *illumination*; Alain, of the *propos.*

Alain, for whom freedom of the mind was the fundamental law of man, could have formulated his thoughts in no other way than to "propose" them for deliberation. Consider also the various devices of style: nothing could be more revealing than their changing modes. It was Mallarmé's genius for allusion and "absence" that transformed the metaphor into the symbol. It was likewise the profound powers of *vision* in Supervielle which at last removed the shutters of concept from medieval allegory.

Several further considerations confirmed my earlier view. From his grammar-school days at Sète in the 1880s until his "crisis of 1892," Valéry had held to the practice of *verse* as the essential mode of poetry. Neither *The Old Alleys*, a prose poem dedicated to Huysmans in 1889, nor the handful of experimental prose pieces of about the same period were at all to be compared with the profusion of sonnets and other poems in verse—some two or three hundred that I know of—which he composed between the ages of sixteen and nineteen and consigned wisely to a drawer. The former were as yet merely fragments of "poetic prose," descriptive or decorative in nature; they in no way foreshadowed his later treatment of the prose poem, the first published example of which was *Pure Dramas* (1892). This was the moment when Valéry had just discovered Mallarmé, and Rimbaud's *Illuminations*, and was laying down the principles of his "method," the purpose of which was to clarify the acts and functions of his own thought.

The silence or rather the half-silence that followed the "night in Genoa" (1892) was not really a case of deserting poetry at all but rather of defining its role in "the great game" of the mind; for, as we now know, the so-called period of silence was frequently interrupted by an output both in prose and verse, which was to remain unpublished and to which I shall return. It shows beyond any doubt that the break with poetry—except, perhaps, with the sort he called "literature"—was at no time decisive.

I was not unaware also that, after the period of *La Jeune Parque* and *Charmes*, Valéry went on to the very end of his life writing in verse. This indeed was his demon. Yet these later poems in no way recall his earlier tireless pursuit of the perfectly realized pure poem. What is astonishing, in fact, is their abundant natural flow of lyric feeling, coming at the end of a poetic output brief in compass and even famous for the rejection of every sort of looseness or indulgence. Neither had I forgotten the verse translation of Virgil's *Eclogues* nor the rough drafts of poems here and there in the Notebooks nor the *Carmina eroticissima* from nearly every period of his life. Valéry had made a collection of the latter and thought briefly of having them printed—in two copies, one for himself, the other for the "Enfer" of the Bibliothèque Nationale. In an incisive preface, he spoke particularly of how difficult it was to find a true poetic speech for so special a genre, where the need for precision and for a degree of realism almost inevitably suggested terms that were either vulgar or too technical—the vocabulary either of anatomy or of the gutter. So far as I know, he never wrote poems of this kind except in verse, feeling perhaps that only the beauties of form and the transfiguring fire of poetry could purify the pudenda of the flesh.

Finally, I confess that I have been particularly struck by the fact that in his critical writings Valéry repeatedly proclaimed his poetic "revelation" and creed. For me, these were the proof of his vocation, which he himself sensed in the second of his given names, Ambroise: a name that to him irresistibly suggested *ambroisie* and *abeille*—"ambrosia" and "bee."

O dieu démon démiurge ou destin
Mon appétit comme une abeille vive
Scintille et sonne environ le festin
Duquel ta grâce a permis que je vive.

(O god demon demiurge or destiny
My appetite like a vivid bee
Glitters and hums about the feast
At which your grace has given me to live.)

Within the confines of formal verse, Valéry had tirelessly pursued the idea conceived in his early youth, of "poetry as music," in which "delightful movement" held sway over meaning and became the generating principle of the "charm" —i.e., poem. He was confirmed in this notion by some of his great predecessors. In numerous critical passages, and throughout the Notebooks with their almost daily inquiries into the nature of poetry, he constantly reaffirmed the creative supremacy of the verse poem over the prose poem. Actually his search for a language capable of producing "constellations of words," led him back time and again to the traditional meters as the only measure of time, the only control of rhythm that could manage a stop or a suspension of movement at the close of a rhyme. According to Valéry it is this decisive rest, partitioning off each line, which creates the inner play between the parts of a line as well as the mutual attraction of sounds forming clusters and connections out of the concrete elements of words.

To be sure, the definition of poetry which he proposed, "the kind of movement that transforms thought into harmonic figures," was equally valid, as we shall see, for the poem in prose. But I could not forget that Valéry himself had for a long time doubted this, insisting repeatedly on "the immortal difference" between the rhythmic structure of verse and that of prose. This difference resided in the fact that in *prose*, deprived as it is of the "whole rest" made possible by meter, each member *tends to go free of the others*.

Now I no longer believe—Valéry himself notwithstanding—that he is to be thought of solely as a poet in verse, nor that his poetic work is to be fully appreciated without his accomplishment in the genre of the prose poem. That would be to underestimate the ambition of his experiment and to see his poetic achievement in a mistaken perspective. For too long the perfection and purity of his verse, his fidelity to the restrictions of orthodox prosody (sometimes taken a bit foolishly as a revival of the classical models), have obscured that other register in which he was no less accomplished. It would have been surprising, in fact, if the possibility of extending the whole range of poetry, which (since Baudelaire) includes the poem in prose, had *not* occurred to a poet so concerned to exercise all the resources of poetic language.

That is not all. Baudelaire was the first in our literature not only to sense the autonomy of the poem in prose but, to say, in speaking of it, that poetry is to be defined not as the creation of beauty but as a form of art. The fact is that the prose poems in his *Spleen de Paris* led, thirty years later, to "the crisis in verse form" and the reaction against traditional prosody which Mallarmé and later on Valéry resisted, but to which both were more deeply sympathetic than anyone has realized. As a result the whole idea of style changed. Modern poetry, like painting and music, found its affirmation in those styles which no longer aimed at ideal beauty but meant to *live* by originality of invention. Just as the development from Manet to Cézanne, or from Monet and Kandinsky to Klee, tended to reduce painting to a world of objects (that is, to its *reality as painting*) and to consider its domain to be simply a number of individual styles, so modern poetry, with Rimbaud, ceased to be merely recitation, amusement, and idealization. The *Illuminations* marked a date of extraordinary importance in the history of French poetry. From that moment, our poets all but abandoned verse. Almost all were to practice a new poetics, no longer that of "poetic" prose nor of mere lyricism in prose, but a new form free of the old prosody, free too of those bastard genres derived from more or less happy combinations of prose and verse. They were all to be indifferent to the quest for "ideal beauty." At times, indeed, they were to show themselves suspicious or even contemptuous of it: "One evening I set Beauty on my knees. And I found her bitter. And I reviled her." They were quick to arrive at a kind of anti-poetry—that is, a poetry bent on rejecting everything that, before, had justified and defined it.

The poem in prose, picturesquely handled by Aloysius Bertrand, developed in depth by Baudelaire and carried to great heights by Rimbaud, has shown itself to be not at all a matter of the false lyricism of poetic prose, but in itself a new kind of poem, endowed with techniques of its own and as far from the verse poem as from pure prose.

The variety of styles it has brought with it must also be considered: each poet has given it his own particular turn. Nothing could be more fruitless than to propose a definition of the genre, pointing to its general structure, its typical features. The prose poems of Rimbaud, the *versets* of Péguy, Claudel, or St.-John Perse, the uphill deep-breathing strophes of Lautréamont, the cadences of Max Jacob or René Char, the *proèmes* of Francis Ponge, though they have in common the character of being neither verse nor poetic prose, are each marked by a tone, a contour, a manner so personal as to be unmistakable. On the shelves of our libraries, they represent as many styles as the canvases of today's painters do on the walls of our galleries, or the compositions heard in our concert halls. To take one example: Claudel's *versets*, instead of conforming to the external laws of traditional poetry, follow the natural measure of breathing, the respiratory rhythm that swells, lengthens, accentuates, heightens, or reduces the volume and speed of each line, according to the intensity, nature, and duration of feeling or thought. It is an art of inspiration and expiration brought back to its source in the rhythm of the breath, an art that in the time and space of the *verset*, inhales, then exhales the life we breathe: like the glass blower and his glass. It is an expressive form created by this poet; it is his own art. For Max Jacob, on the other hand, the poem in prose obeys what he calls laws of situation and transposition. In each of these individual cases, poetry is no longer to be found in modulation and the other devices of style—in the ornamentation which for three centuries had been habitual to French poets; here it is a language of its own, which is to say a language of forms. Its value, its very essence are determined by its style.

Before 1892, Valéry had gone no further than to employ in his prose pieces—lyrical, oratorical, or descriptive—the forms and practices peculiar to the verse poem. At the end of *Paradox on the Architect* (1891) he had used the extreme artifice of inserting, unchanged or almost, the whole of the prefabricated sonnet *Orpheus*, with its flat surface of scarcely camouflaged alexandrines, into the two-dimensional fabric of the prose. Nothing could have been more rash than such a shift from exposition to metaphor, from walking to wings.

But Valéry was soon to give up writing verse in the manner of the Parnassians, and prose muddled with the mysticism of the Decadents. This was the moment of his discovery, about 1892, of the principles that were to govern his own fundamental attitude. At the same time, two events occurred which shook his new-found conviction: he often recalled the shock he had felt on first reading Mallarmé and only a few months later Rimbaud. He had been, so he said, "Intellectually thunderstruck by the sudden appearance of these two extraordinary phenomena on the horizon of his mind." Yet he managed to react against the main thrust of this discovery of "two such highly offensive characters." On the one hand, against Mallarmé who had taken poetry as the center of his universe, Valéry set up his own idol, the Mind, as his principle and center; on the other hand, he found and exposed at the heart of Rimbaud's intelligence a mysticism that tended to dazzle and dissolve the mind in universal light—whereas Valéry, for his own part, was seeking a more and more absolute intelligence, the equal of light itself.

Yet the language of those two creators was not to be disposed of so quickly nor with such self-assurance; the perfection, the intensity of their works drove young Valéry to despair. He believed that in these works he had found "the limits of the art of expression." More particularly, the two corollary aspects of the *Illuminations*, the originality of their structure and their meaning (that is to say, the universality of their theme embodied in the greatest variety of sensory modes, and on the other hand the unprecedented form of the poem in prose, at once *locus* and *formula* of the very vision of the primal all) had astonished him profoundly. "These things were born," he wrote to Pierre Louÿs. Or again: "Only the supreme pages of the *Illuminations*, read at night in the most

xviii

glacial of dreams, can shake me with so unruly but firm a hand. Never before have I so penetrated, re-created, and adored them." There can be no doubt that Valéry's meditations on these crystalline forms of poetry in prose led him to reconsider what until then he had believed, that it was impossible for prose to rise, as verse can, to a form of expression in which all the phonetic and semantic elements chime together and language loses its purely logical character. The *Illuminations* showed him, in fact, the contrary: the creation of a poetic space that was a world in itself, one that without quitting the realm of meaning, could enter the sphere of *resonance*. This was the unforeseeable model. It gave him a sense of the enormous distance as well as the unbreachable wall between poetic prose and prose that is poetry. For Valéry there could no longer be any question of writing prose poems as he had done before, using the resources of prosody—rhythm, rhyme, alliteration, internal assonance and dissonance—nor even, more subtly, of setting up an interplay between these elements, as in verse.

Rimbaud had revealed to him the marvelous resources of prose as a medium at once concrete and abstract, lifted beyond common sense by the power of genius into an almost infinite variety of rhythmic combinations and dissociations, even to the dissonances of primitive harmony. It was in this "diamond-hard prose," more than in Mallarmé's *Divagations* or *Un Coup de Dés*, I believe, that Valéry sensed the possibilities, as well as the advantages for himself and his own discoveries, to be found in a unique form of poetic expression. But we must recognize how far such a temptation went.

It was precisely during the years of his intensive intellectual preparation in the Rue Gay-Lussac, when he was devoting himself to mathematics and physics and to the study of mental phenomena, that Valéry felt the need of a rigorous, abstract language that could express the actual functions and operations of the mind. The time had come when the passionate act of a mind pursuing its own secret was no longer satisfied by his interminable scribbling in his Notebooks, by the light of dawn. This could go on endlessly to no end. True, the very spirit of the enterprise meant rejecting any effort at literary production, even a contempt for books. The intellectual adventure was valid in itself, for its own potential and its *creux toujours futur*; its truth lay simply in going on. But in this kind of "absence" into which Valéry had voluntarily withdrawn there was a living paradox. On the one hand, certainly, was the overpowering drive of his mind, but on the other, the no-less-powerful destiny of his *genius*, which from early adolescence had drawn Valéry to poetry and literature. The stimulus of a method and a grasp of all its possibilities, even with the conviction that such an enterprise must not take the form of literature, could not finally quite stifle his desire to create. His innate creativity and sense of form never ceased, during his celibacies of thought, to visit him with a longing for the literary works he must write. Intellectual activity kept his creativity constantly on the alert. He came to the bold and altogether modern conclusion that *penser* is also *pouvoir*: *to think* is potentially *to do*; at times he even confused the two. Meanwhile, Valéry allowed himself to write *An Evening with Monsieur Teste* and the *Introduction to the Method of Leonardo da Vinci*.

It was at about the same time that the prose poem became the vehicle of his "return" to poetry. The more I reflect on the silence of those twenty years before *La Jeune Parque*, the more I am convinced that the poet was always there in Valéry, but a poet who had chosen another form than verse.

Pure Dramas had given evidence as early as 1892 of his own kind of poem in prose, one that, beyond its intrinsic character, could be recognized in the harmony between its theme—*a thought traced back to its beginnings*—and the amplitude of its rhythmic form. This was the first of a series of more highly finished poems, all related structurally one to another through similarities in rhythm and syntax, musical continuity, and the particular tonal qualities of color and sound. The melodic and harmonic phrasing no longer followed the syntactical structure but the inflection of the voice.

In addition to *Pure Dramas*, there were some thirty poems in prose left unpublished, poems written under the influence of Rimbaud and of Mallarmé's *Divagations*. These were the first compositions in which Valéry had tried to transmute his theories into prose poems. He called them his *theoriorama*. In these poems his attempt was to bring together analytical thought and ecstasy, abstraction and sensuality, in *the mode and movement of prose*. Here the lift and undulation of the words, the powers of imagery and voice, create the unique space of poetry.

The importance that Valéry attached to *Pure Dramas* is obvious: he spoke of this poem repeatedly to Gide, Louÿs, and Fourment long before he sent it to them; he asked for their criticism and apologized for the ending, calling it mere *tautology*. Last of all, on one of those small scraps of paper on which he had the habit of recording for himself, and no doubt for his future scholiasts as well, his notes *In Memory of Myself*, he mentioned for the year 1892, along with his theories of coincidence, imagination, form, and ornament, his *Pure Dramas*.

The allusive arabesque of *Pure Dramas* traces the mind's desire as it returns to its source—to its very first look at the world. We may no doubt find in this poem a nostalgia for the primal light upon the first garden. And if we look further we may recognize the sort of angelism of the mind of which Valéry never entirely rid himself. The mystique of "pure mind" never ceased to evoke in him at moments of intellectual exaltation a dazzling sense of wings throughout all "intelligible space." From *The Angel at the Sepulchre*, which he wrote as a boy, to *The Angel*, written in 1922, a mysterious and faithful messenger of the imagination lighted the dawn skies of his mind and permeated the pure acts of his consciousness, which could never understand the suffering that was a part of its condition:

Je sens peser sur moi la fatigue d'un Ange.

I feel weighing upon me an Angel's weariness.

Even with these reservations, we must still recognize that in *Pure Dramas* the analogy is essentially intellectual. Behind the appearances in which things are caught, there is no miracle except the wonder of nature and the primeval order of her changes—that primal scene in which rhythm itself imparted to water its wave, to the stem its curve, to light its vibration. What the mind is able to imagine of the life of things—movement, reflections, echoes, endless lines—these do not exhaust its image-making powers. The marvel remains—uneasy, uncertain: "One could believe the shimmering garden is about to take flight—and if the moment's flowers sport wings to flee with, where shall we go, Ideas?"

The mind may dream "the pure Drama of a line drawn upon heaven-colored or upon life-colored space! Only in beautiful movement can it exist." Such are "the rarest and most harmonious forms of intelligence, and they would replace all the others by their extraordinary beauty, which longs to endure."

It was with the last of these observations that Valéry, eight years later in *Agatha, or the Saint of Sleep*, was to resume his exploration of the literary region of the mind. Here again he attempted to give the form of the poem in prose to one of his boldest insights into language and the powers of consciousness. Almost fifteen years separate this unfinished masterpiece from his later one, *La Jeune Parque*. Yet a profound kinship joins the two. In fact, the first panel of the diptych of *La Jeune Parque*, though woven of other themes and a different fiction, traces the same anabasis of consciousness up to "the limit of self-suspense." Consciousness in *Agatha*, contained as it were in what has already been, moves back through time to gain access to the "secrets of sleep." In the effort to reach into her own roots, she lets go and drifts through herself as through a dream, observing with heightened attention the successive shifts and variations of her own images and thoughts, to the point of vertigo, where she herself is snuffed out in absolute dark. In *Agatha*, the search for greater and greater "clarity" develops the other way round from the way of light—that is, by the gradual darkening and letting go, in controlled stages, of the functions of consciousness. The movement is backward, tracing the willing effacement and regression of being, back to a thought that has no beginning. "Our Lady of Sleep," lucidly descending as if by stairs into the naked midnight of consciousness, watches over the nocturnal pole of thought. She is already her own "Jeune Parque" spinning the thread of mind, no longer extinguished in light but at the heart of the "living dark," unwinding and snipping the thread of her own destiny. This plunge into the deep night of the mind is similar, though opposite in direction, to the thinker's ascent to the mind's solstice in *Le Cimetière marin*, where consciousness desires to reach the still point of absolute radiance. From midnight to noon, in the world and in the mind, from infinity to zero in thought, between being and nothingness, consciousness attempts to expose itself in turn to the twin splendors of sun and death.

It may be interesting in regard to Valéry's poetic work of that time to consider how, in each case, he worked out the common theme of *Agatha* and *La Jeune Parque*. He had originally written the latter as a prose poem consisting simply of the framework of theory for an intellectual autobiography, with nothing of the fable and nothing of the whole "sexual" element, which were added later on. *Agatha*, on the other hand, was from the first to be constructed around a fiction, with scenes, characters, events, and argument. The idea for a tale came first. Valéry imagined Agatha at the moment before she sits down to dinner: lifting her arms to take hold of a platter, she falls, and her mother finds her stretched out asleep among the débris, etc. This projected fiction soon gave way to a strict study in "transcendental psychology" and along with it another prose poem *Plus je pense, plus je pense* ("The more I think, the more I think") began to take shape. In the latter, nothing of the tale remained but its title.

During the years 1898–1903, intellectual and creative work went on together, but the products of the two remained separate—efforts to join them notwithstanding. A poem in progress would be staked out and attacked by means of a complex apparatus of analyses, notes, comments, and lists— on memory, dreams, sleep, the rise and eclipse of ideas, on pure sensation, etc.—the whole being an imaginary description or experimental projection of the functioning mind, under the sign of the famous adage: *Nihil est in intellectu quod prius non fuerit in sensu*. The mind observes the writer at work and circumscribes both his labor and what he creates. His intellectual probing seems at times to have come before, at other times after, the actual composition of his poems. Sometimes both activities must have gone on at once, or almost. However that may be, the most nearly finished work in this whole group of "documents" is the poem in prose *Agatha*.

Valéry left it unfinished; and therefore left unanswered, this time forever, one question which to my mind is important: what was his idea of the poem in prose—its structure, its technique, its function—during the period 1892–1912 when, thinking that he had turned his back on literature, he yet returned so irresistibly to the one literary form which he felt might "lift into song what has no need of song"—the motions and very acts of thought? He used to say to Gide, about words, that he had often wanted to throw his own boots at their heads, rather than polish theirs. But words were already taking their revenge on him, and were finally to subdue the rebel beyond all prediction. There can be no doubt that he attempted at that time "to construct a literary work in the manner of a vast mathematical operation." But what did he mean by that? "I once dreamed," he tells us, "of a piece of writing in which every thought that went into its making had been clarified—in which every nonessential element of meaning in the words had been removed. . . . More than that I wanted the reluctant reader to be absolutely gripped by those forms designed to take hold, suddenly, of the very mechanism of his thought and to think in his place, there where his thinking is done, just as a man who, if someone takes hold of the two parts of his arm and forces him to make certain gestures, is thus physically compelled to interpret and understand them."

Does the published text of *Agatha* represent such an ambition? Is it one of those texts capable of reproducing in the reader the exact motions of the writer's mind? Does it have that formative power which Valéry dreamed of? It would be difficult to say. On the one hand, having no relation whatever in form to pure mathematics, and on the other, containing no fiction, the poem follows twin itineraries, the one analytical, the other metaphorical; and these develop at times separately, or again combine. The simplest, most abstract expressions quickly change into the full-bodied figures of a rhythmic prose charged with echoes and resonances of every kind. We see the world of the mind transposed into images, into plastic equivalents and the modulations of poetic language. The mechanisms and phenomena of the mind are expressed in analogies, its rhythms in ornament, its thought in reveries and visions.

Baudelaire is known to have dealt with the various drafts of his *Spleen de Paris* in the same manner. He had known by intuition that the prose "poems in the rough," being artistically less finished than that of the verse poem, could adapt to the "fits and starts" of consciousness and bring back from its incursions into the labyrinths of sleep or dream or darkness the most uncommon wonders—or horrors—for its prize. Which would you have: a poetry tricked out with art, or a poetry drawn from life itself? Remember the poor child showing his toy to the rich child: a live rat in a cage! And both "laughing together like brothers, showing teeth of the *same* whiteness." Yet, in spite of his equally profound intuition of the scope and possibilities of the poem in prose, Baudelaire had continually revised the early drafts of his *Spleen de*

Paris which, in their first form, their nudity, their raw immediacy, were the result of outbursts from the chaotic depths, the unfathomable terror of the abyss. He had been unable to refrain from revising them, bringing them, so he thought, nearer to perfection, introducing into their form-lessness the strategies of music and imagery—in short, the resources and certainties of art.

Valéry himself experienced a similar difficulty in handling form: how was knowledge to be turned into poetry, ana-lytical thought into art? How bring together precise think-ing and pleasure, pure consciousness and delight? Yet in that considerable undertaking which was *Agatha*, the only work in which Valéry actually attempted to join the thinker to the poet, his various efforts never quite came together, either from lack of time, or rather, as I think, because he never found the formula that would make them one.

The fact that his *Orpheus* was left unfinished seems to me significant. Written and rewritten continuously from De-cember 1897 to 1901, and again revised in 1920, it was to be a sort of tragic fairy-play. Valéry sketched out the plan, the principal scenes, the action, chose the characters, and then tried—in vain—to write a few fragments of dialogue. Never-theless—and this bears on our point—two monologues, two islands of pure poetry in prose, emerged from the débris of this vast enterprise. Here again we may wonder about the failure of the projected drama and the perfection of these few pages, standing apart from a larger text in which they found no place. The characters created to exemplify the theater of the intellect remained, in *Orpheus* as elsewhere, ineffectual—pure allegories. Valéry never managed to give them either the reality or the illusion of "stage people," whether because he lacked the gift of losing himself to live again in a fictional self, or because the lucidity of his mind made him despise this kind of uncontrolled creativity, or again because his passion for intelligence blinded him to every other end than itself.

He seemed far more at ease with the form of the poem in prose. The fact that he came back to it so often, and compulsively, by way of so many experiments of every kind: "philosophical tales," "brief texts," "abstract poems," "poems in the rough," stories, and all sorts of compositions more or less related to these in form, or mixed (his taste for mixing the genres is well known) ... his persistence in these practices seems to prove that he sensed in the prose poem, more than in any other literary form, the possibility of bringing into harmony both rigorous thought and the figurative means of expressing it. It is here perhaps that this poet's purest creative impulse is to be found. This at least is what we are beginning to perceive, with the gradual publication of the work of his famous "period of silence."

The *ABC* poems and *Calypso*, the latter (in contrast to *The Angel*) standing proudly on the frontiers of sensual expression: these two show in retrospect the direction Valéry was taking from the moment he wrote *Pure Dramas*. The grand manner was to be recognized also, beyond the bounds of the verse poem, in certain pieces from *Mixture*, in one of the *Broken Stories*, or in some simple description (a tiger, a hand, a sunrise, a bird, a glance, a jewel, a tree, a seashell) in which we see and hear the clear diamond-hard crystal forming, giving us a prose poem specifically Valéry's.

One word more. It was at the moment when he was writing his *Fragments of the Narcissus* that the beautiful idea of *The Angel* came to him, not to be finished for nearly twenty-five years. The inclination, or rather the attraction away from the verse poem, is evident; we have only to consider the climate of the fiction and the theme of the incorporeal spirit in both. Narcissus' image in the pool—the reflected self, stripped of the opaque body—points to the analogy of pure mind to be embodied later on in *The Angel*. By a moving conversion, the mind's reflection is made incarnate in a Being of diaphanous body. But the mind as Angel, having full knowledge of itself and all things—the darkness of "the darker half" now gone—looks into its own transparency and cannot understand how, always, it has been "a prey to infinite sadness." The tears of the mind flow at the very heart of light.

Here we come to the root of the mystery, the drama of thought in Valéry—that extreme point of consciousness where the mind's clarity still cannot understand its own "fatal cause." This tear-filled eye of the mind—the ineffable touchstone of all his poetic work—penetrates, like a secret and lustral water, even into the mind's proudest reaches. "So there is something else than light?" sighed the Angel. That an anguish so fundamental should have found perhaps its most perfect expression in this supreme poem, this alone would be enough, I believe, to alter the perspective in which Valéry's poetic work has so far been considered. We cannot henceforth confine it to a single register, the traditional modes of verse; his poetry has in fact another and no less authentic dimension of form, an entirely modern one, the prose poem.

OCTAVE NADAL

POEMS IN THE ROUGH

Parables

To Accompany Twelve Water-
colors by L. Albert-Lasard

> *Suddenly a strident anger runs through*
> *the aviary. They rise astonished and*
> *take off one by one into the unreal.*
> R. M. RILKE, *The Flamingos*
> (Jardin des Plantes)

> *Man is neither angel nor beast.*
> BLAISE PASCAL

When there were no more than Beast and Angel,
And GOD lively everywhere, in that Garden;
The flyers in the air, and on the ground
The crawlers, and in the profound
Soundless abyss the darting shiverers;

When God and Things and Beasts and Angels
And Light the Archangel were all that were:
IT WAS THE EPOCH OF THE PURE.

Pure the Lion, pure the Ant,
Pure the Bull and the Serpent,
Pure the Dragon, pure the Virtues,
Pure the Thrones and the three high Orders;

3   I-2

Pure was the Earth, pure was the Light,
They were all pure,
Each being that which he was,
Each doing that for which he was made,
Faultless and marvelous:

Each the fruit of a Thought of life
Exactly converted,
Without remainder.

AND I, all this I knew
With an utter strange clarity;
And yet was aloof, standing
Apart from my inward word.

And then, as I was this notable distraction,
No longer a someone, no more than my own fraction,
As my mind's eyes reflected this purity,
Receiving as the mirror of a calm water
The balance and brilliance of things without flaw,
Innocent of notion,

Look! from between the leaves came
To light a Figure, a Figure came
Into the light,
Looked all about him,

And he was "neither Angel nor Beast."

THE GLASS of my sheer presence quivered
As the calm of a calm water
Wrinkles to the course of a form,
Or as when from the full depths and the height's
    shadows
Glances without emerging
A creature one never sees.

4

On my enchantment's mirror of virgin duration
Appeared a trembling;
Over the forehead of the pure hour scuttered
A kind of question that bowled like a leaf
The rosy picture; and like a cry,
Like the grip of an unexpected hand,
An unknown power was closing about my heart.

MAN was this event:
Such the name that I give you.

I KNEW, as if within HIM, that he was neither
    ANGEL nor BEAST:
By unexampled suffering I knew him,
Unexampled, unpicturable,
And nowhere in the body;

A wonder of incomparable suffering
As of the sole and insupportable Sun
Whose anguish lights the world. . . .
O pain of the Sun they call joy and splendor,
Your brilliance is a bitter cry, your agony
Burns the eye ! . . .

HE FELT, there was, I sensed it,
A presence of sorrow apart,
Denied to the Pure Existences,
Neither ANGEL nor BEAST can sustain it.

For ANGEL is ANGEL, BEAST BEAST,
Nothing of either is a thing of the other,
There is nothing between them.
But HE was neither the one nor the other,
This I sensed with instant perfect knowledge,
Knowledge of suffering, suffering of knowledge;

And MAN's silence and my silence
Were interchanging spirits instant by instant....

"ANGEL," said in me He whose absolute presence
I had made my own:
"ANGELS," he said to them,
"Eternal marvels of light and love,
Pure acts
O only knowable by desire,
By hope, by pride, by love,
By all that is a presence of absence, You are
Still mysteries that burn
A little higher than my highest I....

"BUT YOU, BEAST,
The more I regard you the more I become MAN
In Mind, O Beast,
And the more you become strange,
For Mind knows only the things that are of Mind.

"IN VAIN by Mind I hunt you,
In vain by Mind set snares
Baited with gifts of Mind:
ORIGIN? PURPOSE? PRINCIPLE? CAUSE?
(Or CHANCE even, and all the TIME that needs)
O LIFE,
The more I think of you, O LIFE,
The less to thought you yield....

"TO DIE, not less than to be born,
Eludes all thought:
Love, death, are not for Mind
That eating amazes, sleeping abashes.
My face is a stranger;

6

The contemplation of my hands
Poses me questions; to their latent powers,
To the numbers of their fingers, no reply.
Not by thought could one divine
The roll call of his members nor their forms:
And yet through them alone I know the Other.

"The happiness of the BEAST is all happy,
A joy without shadow.
He does not and he cannot know
The adulteration of joy with sorrow,
Of sorrow with joy,
Nor the mixing of time with time,
Or of sleep with waking.
No matter how quick to the leaf's least bruising,
He savors the moment, consumes the gift:
Pure he is thereby.

"AND NO REGRETS, remorse, suspicions, care:
 For what is not is not;
What will be is not; and what would be;
What was, what might have been,
They are not. . . .
Nothing departs from order: his mindings backward,
His lookings forward, do not dilute his present.
Pure he is thereby.

"BUT WE!..."

In Praise of Water

MANY have sung WINE.

Innumerable the poets who have lyrically ennobled their drunkenness, pledging the gods in the strong cup their soul has desired.

Most precious WINE, worthy of all praise! And yet the folly and ingratitude of those among them who have spoken ill of WATER. . . .

Divine limpidity, living crystal, marvelous agent of life, universal WATER, I shall offer you unbidden the homage of litanies without end.

I shall speak of STILL WATER, landscape's ultimate luxury, stretching her sheets of total calm in whose pure face the reflections of all things seem more perfect than their origins, and all Nature is Narcissus and with itself in love. . . .

Of MOVING WATER, by sweetness and violence, oozings and usings fabulously slow, by the weight of its currents and unbridled whirlpools, by fog and downpour, by streamlets, waterfalls, and cataracts, fashioning rock, polishing granite, wearing marble, interminably sphering pebbles, lulling and trailing in idle drifts and soft beaches all her finished sand. She works and alters, she shapes and adorns, the sad brutal face of callous soil.

Of MULTIFORM WATER, tenant of clouds, amasser of the abyss: she lies in snow on sunlit peaks, whence issuing pure she goes by tracks she knows, blind but strangely certain, down unconquerably to the ocean where she most abides.

At times, swift, slow, lucid in the light of day she chases herself with a mysterious murmur that alters suddenly into a leaping torrent's bellowing, soon swallowed in the perpetual thunder of shuddering, dazzling falls with circlets of rainbow in their mist.

But at others steals away to travel secret, penetrative, below the earth. She searches mineral beds, picking and winding into them by devious ways. She seeks herself in the absolute night, finds herself and is one. She pierces, rummages, dissolves, sweats through, slides down rock veins, is busy about her fantastic labyrinth in which she is never lost; and then subsides in tombs of lakes she nourishes with long tears that set in marble columns, cathedrals of darkness venting infernal streams that breed blind fishes and shellfish older than the flood.

And in these perilous adventures what strange things WATER has known ! . . . And strangely she knows them. For her substance is her memory: she picks and gathers memorials of all she has brushed against, bathed, in her course rolled—of the limestone she has scooped, the rockbeds she has smoothed, of the rich sands through which she has sunk. When she gushes into day she is charged with all powers and virtues of her traversed rocks. With her she fetches scatterings of atoms, of elements of naked energy, of bubbles of subterranean gas, at times indeed of the very heat of the molten middle earth.

And so she rises, laden with the gleanings of her way, to offer herself to the needs of LIFE.

How not venerate this very essence of all LIFE? And yet how few men understand that LIFE is no more nor less than WATER organized !

Consider a plant, regard a mighty tree, and you will discern that it is none other than an upright river pouring into the air of the sky. By the tree WATER climbs to meet light. Of a few salts in the earth WATER constructs a body that is in love with the day, to the whole universe stretching and out-stretching liquid powerful arms that end in gentle hands.

Man comes to rest where there is WATER. What more necessary than that cool sweet nymph? The nymph and the spring stand at that holy place where life sits down and looks around her.

And here one will understand that there is also a drunkenness of WATER. To drink ! . . . To drink. . . . Well one knows that pure thirst is quenched only in pure water. There is some-thing exact and satisfactory in this matching of the real desire of the organism with the element of its origin. To thirst is to lack a part of oneself, and thus to dwindle into another. Then one must make good that lack, complete oneself again, by repairing to what all life demands.

The very language is filled with the praise of WATER. We say that we THIRST FOR TRUTH. We speak of a LIMPID discourse. At times we burst into a TORRENT of words. . . .

Time itself has drawn from the coursing of water the figures in which it presents itself.

To WATER be all praise!

The Anagogical Revelation

An abstract tale

1. At this date (MDCCCXCII) two terrible angels, Νοῦς and Ερῶς, showed me a way of destruction and of domination, and a fixed Boundary at the far end of that way. I knew the certainty of the Limit, and the importance of that knowledge, which is as valuable to us as the knowledge of the Solid— or (to symbolize it otherwise) may be used analogously to that of the wall against which a fighter sets his back, so that he fears no assault *a tergo* but dares all his enemies equally face to face and so makes it an even contest—(this being the most remarkable feature of this discovery for, amongst his adversaries, he who is *Himself* or those who are the *Person* that he is, with all his diverse insufficiencies, figure as extraneous and adventitious concomitants.

And the two angels, themselves in person chasing me before them, coalesced into one; and I, turning to face them, had but a single power to fight against, once I felt the Wall behind my shoulders.

2. I sought to see this limit and to define this wall.— I wished to "write," both for and within myself, in such a way as to make use of this knowledge, the laws of this limit or sealing-off; or (what comes to the same thing)

those of the reduction to unity of all that is hurled against it; and further those which determine that in the ordinary way we do not perceive these things, but rather that thought builds herself illusory castles on the far side of the Limit, as though the Wall behaves like transparent glass—a thing which I do not believe. A mirror rather: but do not forget that you will not recognize yourself in a mirror unless you see someone else there, and that in this mirror you will not.

The Angel

A kind of angel was seated upon the rim of a well. He looked for his reflection and found that he was a Man, and in tears, and he was dumbfounded at the appearance in the naked water of this prey to an infinite sorrow.

(Or, if one wishes, it was a Sorrow in Man's shape that lacked a cause in crystal heaven.)

This face that was his, the grief that racked it, both seemed alien to him. So wretched an apparition aroused the interest of the fabulously pure spiritual matter of which he was composed; exercising it, asking questions that found no answers.

"O my Evil," *he said,* "what are you to me?"

He tried to smile: and wept. This infidelity of his features confounded his perfect intelligence; they had assumed an air of the particular and accidental, and their expression had become so unequal to the universality of his limpid knowing that he was mysteriously wounded in his unity.

"I have nothing to beweep," *he said*; "nor could that be possible to me."

The Movement of his Reason within the light of his eternal expectancy found itself halted by a nameless query; for what would create pain in our own imperfect natures does no more than arouse questionings in essences that are absolute;—while indeed for us every question too is or will be a sorrow.

"Then who is this," *he said*, "who loves himself to the point of self-torment? I am all-knowing; and yet I see that I suffer. This face is certainly my own, these tears are my tears. . . . And yet am I not that power of clarity of which this face, these tears, their cause and what might eliminate that cause, are but the merest particles of its extent?"

But, in vain did these thoughts grow and multiply in all the amplitude of the sphere of thought, in vain did the similes chime, the contradictions announce themselves only to be resolved, in vain was the miracle of clarity incessantly achieved, with each Idea sparkling in the glitter thrown off by every other, jewels as they are of the circlet of undivided knowing: nothing at all resembling a harm offered itself to his faultless gaze, nothing by which to explain this visage of sorrow, these tears that he saw through his tears.

"The purity that I am," *he said*, "Intelligence that effortlessly consumes all creation, without anything affecting or altering it in return, can recognize nothing of itself in this face of lamentations, in these eyes whose light, of which they were made, is as it were softened by the moist imminence of their tears.

"And how can he so suffer, this lovely weeper who is mine, is of me, considering that after all I see all that he is, being in myself the knowledge of all things, and that the only sorrow could be to be ignorant of something?

"O my astonishment," *he said*, "charming and sorrowing Head, is there then something other than light?"

Thus he questioned himself within the universe of the fabulously pure spiritual matter of which he was composed, and in which all the ideas dwelled equally distant both from one another and from himself, in so absolute a perfection of their harmony and a promptitude of their correspondences that he himself could almost have disappeared, leaving the system of their synchronous ordinance, coruscating like a diadem, to subsist independently in the ample sublime.

And for an eternity he never ceased to know and fail to understand.

Mixture

MIXTURE IS MIND

Prose, poem, recollection, image, phrase,
From sleep what comes, what comes from love, each
   chance
The gods donate by way of circumstance:
Here see the swept-up pieces of my days!

According to its moment droll, nice, rich,
Master of law or servant of a fly,
   Mind is mixture out of which
Each instant disengaged uprears the *I*.

Mixture

I

Glassy sea—gray, with great clotted areas of local activity, curdlings, pins-and-needles of the skin.

Wave is form. Motionless, of moving substance; or moving, and its matter "still."

"A wave"—in what is that an *identity*? It is a continuum of forms and movement. A light upon a turning but invisible wheel, and a series of points in a circle lighting up one after the other are not distinguished by the *eye*. *Duration always* involves both "space" and "time."

II

Stones rolled by the sea, and the same worked upon in air by frosts and rains, belong to different classes of form. These are not comparable wearings: they do not share hazards. The action of the sea is various: that of weathers and gravity not. The one is rolling and hurling: the other lashes, cracks, picks apart.

III

A crest of foam in the wide plain of the sea *from time to time*
catches the light: these *times* too are the creation of chance.

IV

Morning—black blowy dawn—cannon-shots of wind
Notable tension of the nerves
Remarking, reverberating at, the least event, alteration—as
      onto the loaded present *issued from sleep*
Of resonance, illumination, expectation,
Three-quarters slumberous, and the rest a point vibrating.
Fine waves, potent, but pent in a little space.

THE CATHEDRAL

Windows of Chartres—lapis, enamels. The Orient.

Ingredients of some complex drink, the innumerable little
elements of *living* color (that is to say, emitting a radiance not
polarized, not reflected, but a mosaic of intense tones),
sharply divided and in every possible juxtaposition *inch by
square inch*, produce a soft dazzle that is more of a taste than
a sight, the delicate intricacy of the designs allowing one to
see or to not see them—*ad libitum*—or to see only combina-
tions picked out by unusual frequencies, here of blues, here of
reds, and so on.

A look of grains, stones of miraculous jewelry, cellular,
seeds of the pomegranates of paradise.

Effect of other world.

A rose-window puts me in mind of a huge expanded retina, suffering under the diversity of the vibrations of its living elements, color-producers....

Certain prose phrases of Mallarmé are such windows. Their subjects could not matter less, they are caught and drowned in the mystery, vivacity, depth, laughter, reverie of each separate fragment, each one feeling, singing....

Right porch—the middle one not good, the figures imbecile—the left spire unpleasing.

AT GRASSE

I

Slow sounding of bells.

Frog-noise, twittering of birds.

The croakings regular as saws, descanted by the chip and chisel of the birds.

Scents. One cannot tell whether of gardens or of perfumeries.

II

I see, in the very center of my window's square, a man grubbing his field. Pace by pace he edges forward in his task, bent, planted by his two legs in the soil: white shirt, blue trousers: he strikes, and then he puts his hands in the earth.

He is at such a distance that my littlest fingernail hides him entirely.

He is the pivot of the countryside that I see extending about him, rising in crest upon crest to the mountains, from fawn wave to blue wave, bearing sharp little houses, flocks of olives, black needles that are cypresses.

This is France, and the little figure with the pick is perhaps French. There is one chance in three that he is Italian. He labors, there are men who need what he is doing there.

Here is another peasant, thumbing the fly off his roses, arched in shirt sleeves, in a crowd of birds that take off under his nose, then drop upon the tip or leader of a cherry tree.

Soft color and aspect of that house built like a temple, guarded by olives; its bleached limestone scattered with dawn-rose, ocher, creams; the gentle slope of its roof, the tiles spotted with rust and tan; the obtuse angle of the gables, the gray-blue shutters; the mighty cypresses set in threes.

Not long ago it belonged to Maeterlinck.

The man with the pick—specialized machine—feet well planted in the thick soil. He lunges: and then the struggle to drag out the blade, straighten the head and body from the waist, raise the whole massy torso: and then again, and again. The silence and the panting of that laboring man.

III

Out of a landscape that is twilit still
A house, a single flowering almond tree,
Grow golden, conjuring up the sun
I cannot straightly see;
And then out of a dusk of shrubs and bushes
A great tree lights with flame, shaking
In the cold dawn wind
Groupings of groupings, a whole disorder

Of delicate detail, winnowing them out
From the heap of its green light. And then the olive trees
Are born to their fine-spun outlines, brushed with silver:
And Judases show off insipid pink.
Enter the red-tiled roof.
Enter the frizzled masses of the pines.
Enter the hills.
All enter, with the shadows that define them.
The sketch becomes precise: the parts divide,
Each lively in itself; and every theory
Receives the demonstration of a proof.
Each leaf distinct.
Each object separable, no doubts. . . . Each thing
Accepts the proper label of its name.
This teasing-out of all that had to come. . . .

MONTPELLIER

Extraordinarily pure air. The *light* holds rigid this *stone* place,
its gardens, masses defined by sharpness of edge.

At the end of the vertical slit made by this alley between
the gray delicately-shaded petrifaction of the houses, appears
like a jewel, an enamel plaque, a pretty blue mountain set
about with pines.

GENEVA

Fireworks.

Startled swans on the lake of lighted boats, and the marvelous sables of the skies and waters ripped dazzlingly *when least expected* by exquisite rockets that climb, cry, gesture, writhe, and at last resplendently expire.

TIGER

London—tiger in the zoo—a superb animal, a head of formidable solemnity and that mask *one knows*, in which there is something Mongolian, regal force, potentiality, an occult look of power, of something that has gone past cruelty, fatality rather; the features of a truly *absolute* monarch at rest; bored, perilous, loaded: *impossible to be more completely tiger than that.*

Yet this splendid beast crosses, uncrosses, his limbs; from time to time one sees muscles flexing gently under that fulvous mantle streaked with black. The tail is alive. Is he aware of these far displacements? The beast is a sort of empire.

The "sparking-off" of local reflexes—must attempt to decipher the life locked within.

I was unable to stay longer to study this animal, the most beautiful tiger that I have seen....

I think of "literature" *in posse* upon this subject.... Of the images that would be searched for—but not by me: for I should seek to possess him as he is, in the livingness of impermanent form that his every act unforms, reforms, before turning him into letters.

Pendulary motion of wild beasts along the grills where their stripes rub the bars.

He opens his jaws. *Yawns*—presence and absence of the tiger's soul, eternally waiting for something to happen.

THE SAME

The enormous beast lies pressed against the bars of his cage. In his immobility I cannot move. His beauty turns me to stone. I fall into a contemplation in front of this inscrutable animal person. In my mind I assemble the forms and forces of this magnificent pasha, wrapped in a robe so noble and so lithe.

To all he surveys he brings an incurious eye. Artlessly I seek to read human attributes into his marvelous mask. I cling to that expression, as of a self-contained superiority, of power and indifference, that I find in the features of this absolute ruler—a face strangely veiled, a spidery lace of black delicate arabesque scribbled upon its golden fur.

No fierceness: something altogether more formidable—an inexpressible certainty of being deadly.

What fullness, faultless egoism, sovereign isolation! The imminence of all that he is worth is upon him. This creature makes me think vaguely of a great empire.

Impossible to be more oneself, more exactly armed, endowed, charged, instructed in all that concerns being perfectly tiger. Every appetite, temptation, finds its perfect instrument in him ready to hand.

I give him this motto: NO PALAVER.

AUTUMN

Dead leaves. The forest *fairer* for its autumn death, its colors more various, more resonant, than in life.

Is one to speak of "nature" here? These things are dead and dying, this splendor comes *as it may*, from the down-leveling of organisms from which the life has fled.

It is ruin, rotting, rusting that fill our eyes with affirmations that are clear and strong.

"Who has done it?"

These things undo themselves.

And I fall into a study upon *doing* and *undoing*, that I should call "philosophical" were I ignorant that there is no such thing as philosophy, only variations within a closed system upon the senses of words. . . .

CHILDHOOD AMONG SWANS

I was an infant beginning to walk. My nurse would bring me every day to a public garden, overhung with steep banks and jutting rocks, where there was a pool ruled over by a fierce cast-iron Neptune, whitewashed and equipped with a trident.

This pool was inhabited by swans. One day my nurse set me down at the pond's edge, and I played at throwing pebbles into the black water with all the clumsiness of a baby swathed in a cloak with stiff-starched collarettes.

The nurse went away for a moment into the shrubbery where a soldier was waiting, burning with love.

The baby had a large head and weak legs. How could it not have fallen into the water?

There it is, floating among the swans, buoyed up in its starched dresses forming pockets of air.

The nurse and the soldier, having tenderly vanished, were oblivious of the great peril threatening my little destiny. And the swans were surely astonished to see this curious swan in their midst, white like them, but a make-shift swan beginning to sink, for its collarettes and its dresses and its cloak were soaking. The child was already unconscious.

Why did someone see him?

The worst was over. . . .

The man quickly stepped into the water, frightened away the swans, and resuscitated the pale ME that had fainted.

He carried it home, gave it a swallow of rum.

My grandfather wanted to kill the nurse.

DIAMONDS

I

A ballerina: cascade of pirouettes, of a marvelous precision, *brilliant as the facets of a diamond. . . .*

Thirty-two pirouettes! (Karsavina)

A very fine image.

II

Diamond. Its beauty results, I am told, from the smallness of the critical angle of total reflection. . . . The cutter polishes the facets in an arrangement such that a ray of light entering

the stone by one of them can leave it again only by the same
—whence the fire and brilliance.

Fine image of what I believe of poetry: the reissuing of the
spiritual ray through the same words by which it entered.

III

Beauty speaks or sings and we do not know what she is
saying. We make her repeat it. We would listen to her for-
ever. We would breathe her sweet smell forever. We would
gaze forever upon the face and form of the one who is
beautiful. In vain we would seize and possess her, for our
desire has neither bound nor solution. What could perfect
the sensation aroused by what is perfected in itself?

One could write the story of a man sent mad by the beauty
of his mistress—from whom he obtains all (her love, and
every privilege) and yet nothing that love gives can quench
his strange thirst at the sight and notion of her; for nothing
stills it *nor can still it ever*. It would turn upon that.

INTELLIGENCE

I

Intelligence is the power to bring to the act of the present the
resources of the past and the energies of the future.

II

An intelligence perceived that his state was about to cease:
he was to fall from eternity into Time, and become flesh.
　"You are going to *live*!"
　It was *dying* for him. What a horror! To fall into Time!

HUSH!

An admirable title . . .
　indeed in itself a whole admirable Tome!
Better than an "*opus*" . . .
　and yet . . . yes . . . an opus:—"*Because,*"
If you work out (each time
　the form, the motion, of a word
　like a wave
　swell to the destined curve)
From what sensation,
　what recollection, what surprise it arises,
　from what of a presence, an absence; what good, ill;
　born from what nullity, what universal:
And add, observe, take readings,
　compute what counterpoise will hold it
　and the weight of what weight you will load on your
　　tongue,
　and the strain on the rein of will:
You will know power, you will know wisdom,
　and to hush *will be finer far*
　than the army of smiles and the rivulets of pearls
　of which most prodigal is the mouth of man.

THE EMPTY AND THE FILLED

I set down the book; I look at my familiar things, I stroke my chin; I leaf through these notes. And all this passes without impediment, as if freely, as if these were separated and independent events, isolated in the *void*, and without interaction of the one upon the other. And the book lying *there* and the hand resting *here* have no interconnection; no more than the gleaming doorknob has with anything else around it.

But then I can suddenly *see* quite otherwise, and *see with full volition*, that all these things are cogs of a single engine, jigsaw pieces; and that each displacement is inescapably a substitution, as in a liquid in which one molecule cannot be moved without another taking its place. Now nothing is casual, nothing is alone. The independence of objects is now only an appearance. Their apartness, their noncontact, are appearances. And my illusion of *liberty*. . . .

AWAKING

How long have you slept, my friend?

I have slept long enough to change night into day and the darkness into light. . . .

Long enough to know no longer who I was or shall be, but must wait until I can be what I am—he who will take up again in resignation or in joy the burden of my "story" and of my obligations, my bondage and my powers, my face. . . .

MIXTURE

All those elaborations of myself which are myself. And
MYSELF: who may that be?

*

How long have you slept?

I do not know the hour. How should I know it? The cable
parted: *terra firma* sank: contact lost, no signals.

Waking, I disembark. I do not know where I have been
during this voyage, without aim, companions, route, look-
out, that brings me where I was and where I am.

SKETCH

The bird twitches his wings, launches, and in a moment has
lifted his awareness from a branch, and is away. With him he
bears the center of a "world" and ferries it off to be set down
elsewhere. (Whether or no he chooses the branch he lands on,
I am quite ignorant.)

APHORISM

Sunset is feminine.

MOTTOES

For a sundial
LUX DUX

*

For a library
CHOOSE NOT BROWSE

*

For a dream
PLEASE OR CEASE

*

He who smiles and holds his tongue
Sees a shadowy hourglass hung.

A HAUNTED ROOM

"This room," says the man with the key, "looks on to the sea."

Liar. It is not the sea. This room looks on to the infernal fire. The whole sun leaps up at it from that vast mirror that must be the bay, striking the looking glasses, burning anew in every scrap of crystal or metal, until one thirsts for shadows.

The man goes. I close everything, in the hopes of seeing something with my light-bruised eyes.

But, instead of seeing, smell.

This sumptuous apartment has an occupant already, it is pervaded by a perfume that is altogether too rich; a suspicion at first, then an astonishment; tormenting, haunting, bewitching in the end.

From a certain small drawer of the dressing table, if I open it, it emerges with staggering power, dilating the nostrils, distending the cavities of the chest, breathing a presence in absence, a longing for a one not there. It creates women; or woman. From this drawer curls out an essence of intimate hell.

St. Bernard taught us, *Odoratus impedit cogitationem*, Scent inhibits thought. He perceived in odors great temptations. That is because an odor is breathed with our breathing, insinuating itself into the very stuff of life. It becomes life. If it is fragrant, one cannot prevent oneself from seeking it in the air, in every breath of existence; nor from speculating on its source, constructing this out of images which are desirable, unsettling, tender, absurd.

I founder in this perfume that conjures up scenes too living by far.

INTERIOR

Frightful weather; wind and rain at once.

But I am on this side of the glass that they attack, between walls, in the dry and warm. My attention seizes on the storm, then lets it go to fix upon a matter of the mind *that speaks in me*; a moment so, then turns again to the confusions of the sky. How many Days and Works have gone toward allowing thought thus to take shelter, *survive*, grow supple, lose and refind itself, to be prolonged; to gather momentum, to become more than a mere snatched interval between two bodily cares!

MAGIC

"Close your eyes," says the man. "Good. Now, imagine Irma! *Strongly*, clearly. You see her? Good. Now, open them!"

There was Irma before him.

(*Curtain*)

A DREAM

A woman with me in a *clear* country. We see a derelict building, quite *clear*. Water runs toward its gaping door, over a great square doorstone, *clear* water that, the threshold passed, at once runs down over steps, covers them, grows deep. The woman hurries me in. We walk in the already waist-high water and go down, the torrent bearing us through to another door and the day again—a huge lake into which the water falls. The lake is *clear*, with a marvelous limpidity, exceedingly deep. We swim far out into this *clear* water, of very *clear* and luminous green. Pale light. We see the bodies of swimmers. I am struck with fear and wonder at these *clear* deeps filled with legs of an astounding freedom and whiteness. *At the bottom* of the lake, a shining green country, bathed in soft sun, and pale still sand.

THE POET'S SHOP

One sees him through the plate glass, in his blue dressing gown, his face as changeable as the weather. Sometimes young, sometimes extremely old.

He is working, and people stop for hours to watch him. . . . No one sneers. Behind him is the big carved wooden wheel, turning now in this direction, now in that; and sometimes so quickly that the spokes become a blur, and sometimes very slowly indeed.

It is the wheel of words.

On the white paper before him his eyes throw a beam of light, illuminating his hand as it sidles and the stylus it holds traces letters.

One sees him beating time with his head. . . .

SEASCAPE

I

Here the sea gathers again her innumerable dice and throws them.

II

Out to sea I observe through my telescope, and I salute far out, wave number—?

(But only the creator knows the serial number and the biography of this *personality*—for me so swiftly here-and-gone—that, in its own consciousness, has doubtless steadily *lived out* the full *ordinary cursus vitae* of its kind....)

Between each point X, Y, Z, and the coast, *Form* that flies and flees, leaving to its heirs at that point both its shape and its material.

"THE THINKER"

To talk to oneself
   is not very often very amusing:
To make the conversation amusing,
   interesting, instructive, unexpected,
   is to become—a *thinker*.
Rôle of the inner voice.
   Philosophical systems sort ill with
   the natural temper of this *conversation* and
   are at bottom mere *writings*.

EYE

Rapid, vagrant, irresponsible, irrepressible seat of vision, so many times swifter and more sentient than the body, than the very head even; drawn, driven, dodging, and settling like a fly; glutton of objects, winkler-out of ways, coupler of things apart; more volatile member of the less volatile frame, now in thrall to every distraction, now inward fixed communing with the being: it chases over the world, lost sometimes in an object only to find itself once more in darting away.

MOMENTS

I

Nice—almost destarred sky, except one lingerer refulgent in the void. I do not know which. It seems near the ecliptic, a planet surely.

There is a modification of night which is not yet dawn.

The landscape splendid, noble.

Winking shipmarks, the articulations of the town, pricked out in lights.

Man *weighs* what he sees; and by it he *is weighed*.

When he is found too light to match the something in the other pan, a something he cannot flee, then that is the condition of *beauty*.

I consider a poem of the Intellect.

II

Dawn—it is not the dawn: but the dropping of the moon, gnawed pearl, ice melting, a dying gleam the day replaces pace by pace. This pure moment I love, of ends, of beginnings. Of calm, renouncement, negation.

Relinquishment. Deferentially we put back night in its box, fold it, tuck it in. Waking is the drowsy bedtime of what in me is most alone. Sleep itself will sleep, and dreams yield to the dream we call real. Agitation, animation, are born. Muscles, machines, invade the landscape of the self. The real hesitates meanwhile.

The oriflamme is unfurling, and at a whistle-blast will shoot to the yardarms, twig-ends, roofs, and fill the sky.

III

Grasse—thin snow on the ground—not on the trees—
Breughel effect. The earth smudged, not covered.

Sun this morning.

At once chilly and golden sensation, a feeling of childhood.
Elation and sadness mixed.

IV

Grasse—quarter past ten. Suddenly a fine blue and golden
swallow hurls itself into my room, three times circles, finds
the small square window again and escapes, as though
cleaving the image of the landscape open, through that hole
of light which had before been entered as a hole of darkness,
and which an about-turn had sufficed to transform into
radiance, into a quite other world. . . .

Perhaps it did not even recognize it?

V

Here are trees, flowers, a dog, goats, the sun, the peasant and
myself, the distant sea; and we all of us agree that there is no
past.

VI

It is in my own way that I see nature. I think of this while
watching a big goat in the olives. She nibbles, leaps. *Virgil*,
I was thinking. Never would the notion of painting or
celebrating this goat have come to me.

Virgil shows that one could make something of her.

So I observe her. At once she ceases to be a goat; and the olive to be an olive tree. At this point begins *I*—that is to say, my private image that I would wish to exactly define.

A LADY'S FACE

A millionth part of suffering; two thousandths of query; various trace-elements of cunning, greed; a disdain in the nose; a mixed bag of rudimentary emotions skulking behind, or pinned on, the mask.

How, where, when, could all this be got together?... What it adds up to is a "pretty woman."

SEASCAPE

Over the flats of sleep glides in the sea. . . . Listen! The evenness of the tilt, the advance, the exact measure of the beats!

These slow powers win you. Into the sand your limbs and body, with a dead weight, weigh. Your eyes are in the sky, your mouth wide open.

All of you belongs to everything; insensibly grow strange your memory, loves, problems, in the end your self.

The repetitive monotone of the rolling of the soft swell handles and endlessly polishes the projections of your soul, as under the waves it handles and endlessly polishes the pebble's marble.

IDEAS

...There are days "made" for ideas.

On such days ideas arise at the least occasion, from nowhere, indeed from NOTHING.

Nothing precedes, foretells, demands them....

Perhaps (in respect of their origin) they are mere "local" incidents, that would come and go with no more mark than a gleam of foam upon the sea were it not that, this day, the mind is, as it were, "sensitized" to such and such an order of possibilities?

Perhaps there is no perception that can have no *value assigned* to it, be recognized as not usable—but it is up to the mind to divine and then prepare a soil for it: that complex of precise measures, and of the judged effects of such measures, in which, only, this seed may prosper?

My days for ideas are therefore days of as yet uncounted *riches*, riches as yet unassigned, of my thinking self's estate—like the free *available energy*, as yet unemployed, of the horse who paws and would be away.

GODS

It was to call upon himself blessings that the sun-god invented sneezing.

... The end of the world....

God turns over and says, "I have been dreaming."

"After all," said Jove to Jehovah, "you never invented thunderbolts!"

Man, is he worth putting a God to the trouble of "creating" him?

What strikes me most about religion is ... its impurity. Jumble, and more than a jumble, of history, myth, logics, canon, poesy, justice, sentiment, the social, the individual. . . .

More than a jumble: a compound. And that is where it derives its power, and what makes it a force of "nature," as if it were a growth. And that is how it can offer to each of a diversity of beings a unique hand for the mutual grasp.

AT JEHOSHAPHAT

A "spirit" separated from its "body," would it recognize it, O Timotheus, amongst a thousand others?

Would you recognize this arm or skull, so long called yours? Or even your own story?

And too, what could one recall of one's existence prior to the acquisition of language?

AMOR

I

Love excites what remains in us of the "primitive." And it would be an interesting task to show Love, with all its superstitions, rites, and strange constructions, insinuating itself into some being as far removed as possible from the primitive, there to develop in coexistence with the sterilized analytical blade of his mind.

II

Women are fruits. There are peaches, pineapples, nuts. No need to pursue it: that much is clear. The enthusiast cannot resolve to limit himself to a single species. He wishes to learn himself in the diversity of the garden.

III

Amare—imitare. Amative—imitative. One learns it. Words, deeds, "feelings" even: all *learned*. The rôle of books and poems. Original love must be the rarest thing in the world.

Whence the idea for a story. Warfare of the interior, someone's conscience and his intelligence against a torturing love whose force he clearly sees to derive from the conventional, the traditional . . . and he *has a horror of the second-hand*.

IV

It is the *unknown* element that confers *infinite* value upon objects, living or otherwise. Books, paintings, etc.

If this element goes (in "love," for example), what remains conserves only the limited interest of a chase, a diversion; of which one well enough knows how long it will last, what will result, what will come *after*—in a word, its nullity.

V

Desperate love is the sense of the Impossibility of the existence of the loved—so moving, so ravishing; exciting such joy, so fascinated a greed: it is a marveling at an infinity of immaterial connection *compassed into the material finity of a thing*, at a treasure-house of the sensory that, no matter how drawn upon, remains inexhausted. And so on. By the same token, this unlikelihood come to life takes on the aspect of a god. Sensual satisfaction is no more than a more or less happy detail in the relations of idol and idolater, not the indispensable event that it is in cases of ordinary love.

"Is it possible that you exist? *You do.* Inconceivable miracle! *You do*, and this oversets all that I am, alters all values, turns the stones about you to gold, colors the dead and dull, makes as nothing the way to you and the steps and difficulties of the way, measures time with you and time away from you with measures that are not the same. All things are ordered to your tune. The weather of your brow is an all-transfiguring comet, darkening or dazzling the day. Etc.

"What in you gives you that power? No reply. You are ugly; but you are fair. You say nothing out of the ordinary; but no genius can tell me as much as the least word of your mouth."

So the strange power is born and grows in the lodestone, and is as if anterior to every law. One can project no causation that would account for it, no "explanation" to usurp the mystery's place. ... As when a dog runs after its shadow, so enjoyment of presence, contact, and possession fall forever short of the craving for presence, contact, and possession.

The image and idea of the other become more real than the reality of the other.

"You exist. ... You are," says Love, and his eyes grow wide in his astonishment, his inability to believe that the being so absolutely hoped, desired, and necessary should actually take flesh, should be at the same time both idea and creature, his own invention and the gift of fate. And one notes this oddity, that it takes *faith* to believe in the existence of what exists, to accept the being, and the being-there, of this object beyond price; just as it takes faith to conjure up a substance, a virtue, for some truly bodiless fantasy of hope or of despair.

VI

Nothing is more exquisite than the blending of mind with life, of the free creativity of the intelligence with the functional activity of the system. These are two things that one is always tempted to dissociate and mutually oppose. But a good meal enlivened with words and ideas makes us as gods (indeed perhaps better than gods). So it is with the blending of mind with love.

VII

The blending of Mind with Love is the headiest of all drinks.

Age adds its distilled bitters, its black clarities, conferring an infinite value upon the transient drop.

VIII

LOVE, eternal sculptor of the selfsame group!

THE OYSTER

The oyster opens like the *Mimosa pudica*, like a mouth of surprise.

44

PSALM Y

Suddenly on you my hand, prompt, powerful, will fall.
I shall take you by your nape that is full and round,
At the base of knowledge and will, between mind and spirit.
By the support of your rebellious head
I shall hold you, by the pivot of your attention;
Toward what I will I shall press you, and you do not will,
Toward what I will that you will;
Under my feet broken and fair I shall place you and say that
  I love you.
By the neck I shall ply you until I am understood, well
  understood, all understood,
Because I am your Master and your Lord.
You will weep, you will groan;
You will search for indecision in my gaze;
You will lift, you will wring your begging hands, your
  beautiful hands that are most begging, white hands chained
  to your eyes.
You will grow white, then red,
Will smile, seize in your naked arms the strength of my legs,
And you will love me, and you will love me,
Because I am your Master and your Lord.

PSALM Z

My satisfaction is a phantom; never will you achieve it.
Has not the Eternal *created its own offender?*
Has it not formed him of its willed foreknowledge?
Has it not called him into a garden?
Has it not taken a flesh the better to know him?
Your eyes and movements were of a serpent that charms a
serpent.
Roses scented her cheeks and veils.
They have been in the furthest arcana of the night.
To silence they have offered up a sigh.
They have knotted the dying day to the day that is born,
with the knot of their limbs.
They have known their oneness; they have joined their
forces: long have they breathed one another.
And they will not know one another ever.

A MATTER OF EMPLOYMENT

A strong young man was considering his "life" in the light
of day. It was warm and fine. In the sunlight he was flooded
with his own vigor. He breathed superbly; in the weight of
his muscles he was aware of the ripeness of his strength, he
was aware of the springs of action locked in the negligent
abandon of his repose. He thought with a sort of gaiety of
his brutal vigor, of the resources of his arms, of his loins, of
his quick mind and eye. His body and soul, he had them fair

46

and free and at his leisure. Smiling, he considered his life, his horizon, all that he could be and all that at that moment he was, eyeing them in the sun like a good sword well in hand.

What to do with all that?

PATHOS

I

At my feet is the future of the object that I hold and shall let fall. I see at my feet the fragments of the vase.

II

Life prepares continually what she devours continually.
   She consumes beings in the group, and being individually.
   Life devours being.

III

One can listen and not hear.
   It is silence. . . .
   Silence too plays its part in the *universe of the heard*. There are hours, there are places their silence makes notable.
   The ear expands, grows more and more awake in these empty spaces.
   Music can place them.
   There are other silences. They have their function in the *universe of a situation*; in a dialogue where suddenly a response is lacking; in the birth of a love, the ruin of a hope. . . .

IV

Everything happens as though most of existence did not exist. One could define someone by means of what was non-existent for him. . . .

V

Moths—their crazy dance over the dazzling globe.

They cast themselves into the flame as if in desperation, and up flies a pinch of glowing ash. . . .

VI

Ideas as pains.

Our ideas are our own and yet strangers, as are our own and yet strangers the pains that traverse us.

VII

A train halted before the signal, stationary, blackly shining, fuming and consuming at a standstill is the perfect image of waiting.

PSYCHO-BODY POLITIC

I

My physical being is a matter of high policy.

In every man's own personal Constitution a sort of Administration figures, concerned with his *over-all* self-interest, real or conceived.

Thus to *feed*, to *rest*—these are *affairs of State*.

The government (for what it is worth) is the psyche that manages the State and fancies it controls it—a fancy that is inadmissible except when these affairs are elementary, habitual, etc. It is poorly informed. And it can deal only with simple communications, whereas the actual country is frightfully complex. Its province is only such *affairs of State* as are fugitive—love affairs, business affairs, crises of self-conceit.

Proper *affairs of State* are defined as those that excite a profound sensitivity of the being with regard to them: all the departments of sensibility are aroused and *tuned* to act as resonators at the slightest warning. And more: this slightest warning may be infinitesimally small, so that any sort of tremor, *having even no other connection than the I*, any mere *perception* of the I, will arouse some hypersensitive notion, and, as though by spontaneous reaction, set up a disturbance and an intense awareness. . . .

This all happens as though we had within us a *second person*, solely devoted to this particular affair, yet with plenary powers over all—" all " being the sum of everything that is occurring now. . . .

II

To tend. To look after someone, that is also a matter of politics. It can be done with a hand of iron, for which gentleness provides the necessary velvet glove. An exquisite attentiveness to the life that one protects and directs. An unceasing exactitude. A kind of elegance of act, a surveillance and a lightness of touch at once, a foresightedness and a kind of farsightedness that descries the minutest and most distant signal.

It is a sort of opus, a poem (such as has never been written), that intelligent solicitude composes.

MOUTH

The body desires us to eat, and it has built us this succulent theater of the mouth, all lit up with taste buds and papillae. Above, as grand chandelier of this temple of taste, it has suspended the bedropped avid hollows that lead from the nostrils.

The buccal space. One of the oddest inventions of the organism. Dwelling of the tongue. Seat of reflexes, of various degrees of persistence. The areas that taste are discontinuous. Multipurpose machinery. There are fountains and furniture.

And the bottom of this gulf with its treacherous trapdoors, its snapshots and critical nerviness. Preambles and proclamations—this irritated fur, the Tempest of the Cough.

It is a hell-gate of the Ancients. If one were to describe without naming names this cavern, ingress of matter, what a tall tale !

And finally Speech. . . . That huge phenomenon of the deep, with its shakings, rollings, explosions, rhythmical mutations. . . .

ALONE

I

One knows that one is alone and oneself, and wholly so, by the casualness and incoherent particularity of the thoughts that visit one, accompanied as they are by not the remotest will to relationship either with other persons or with their own conclusions.

So one is what one is, a local fact: one can look at oneself (or picture oneself) as a dog looks at a book.

II

NARCISSUS. To look in a mirror, is not that to think of death? Does not one gaze at one's perishable part? The immortal sees its mortal. A mirror takes us out of our skin, out of our face.

Nothing can bear its double.

Repeat a word three times.

III

A tear that is born of your blood at the instant of your grief, running down your cheek in ignorance of the price of its purchase, astounds the mind, which cannot conceive the how and wherefore of this alchemical transmuting. . . .

For it is characteristic of mind to remain ignorant of all such parts of life as do not appear to assist its own workings.

IV

Watch out! He who speaks in your heart is as ignorant as you are.

THE VISIONARY

The angel handed me a book, saying, "It contains everything that you could possibly wish to know." And he disappeared.

So I opened the book, which was not particularly fat.

It was written in an unknown character.

Scholars translated it, but they produced altogether different versions.

They differed even about the very senses of their own readings, agreeing neither upon the tops nor the bottoms of them, nor upon the beginnings of them nor the ends.

Toward the close of this vision it seemed to me that the book melted, until it could no longer be distinguished from this world that is about us.

SINGULARITIES

I

It was a man's opinion or intuition that there are no *similars*, that nothing is ever repeated or matched. A liquid drunk gives no two identical mouthfuls. He found only singulars. He found that three and four have nothing in common and that "two times one" is without meaning. Everything fresh and virgin always. If a memory came to him, he perceived it as a new creation, he apprehended its originality—in that a memory, though "of" the past, is not the past but is an act of the present.

Surely "Nature" works like this. No *past* for her, no repetitions and doubles such as our own gross senses persuade us to admit—our poverty of equipment, our need for simplification.

Yet without this poverty, this need, this falsification, there would be no *intelligence*, no *analogy*, no *universals*.

II

Nothing appears more singular to my eyes, this morning, than that objects should go on as they do, that "bodies fall," that there are things that look like laws, sure consequences, constancies, periodicities; that reasoning is really rather often valid.

This sensation of oddity was my waking creation.... It was my response to things as they are, or as they become again—as if I had expected quite another world. Indeed ... as if it had lain within my grasp.

Assume such a waking, my astonishment: what could be the greatest surprise of all, when one's eyes opened?

III

An object, one day, failed to fall. Alone of its kind, it remained suspended there, a yard above the ground.

No one understood this at all. They built a temple round it.

IV

Two idiocies: The idiocy of assuming a consequential universe. And the idiocy of assuming the reverse.

V

"How singular is a thing that is good!"

This scent—this thick cream—the turn of this neck; and, of my hands, their gliding downward by way of the shoulders onto the breasts, until they form the torso's mass beneath them by a seamless gentleness of touching, a sequence of

altering pressures in my fingers, of firm or of slipping con-
tacts, which make the spirit itself the creator of what offers
itself to this act, moving from place to place and from better
to better. I make you and I remake you. I cannot *resign* this
best of actions, ceasing the melody of my hands. . . .

PSALM S

In the beginning was the Unpredictable
And that begat Antithesis:
And then appeared Oscillation
That led to Apportionment:
And last Purity
Which is the Goal.

BIRDS

A vast nation of little birds appears in the storm sky. Low
clouds wildly dragged by southwest wind; an infinite number
of these birds, come from who knows where, assembling
there in squadrons, forming an army, a body of winged ele-
ments, performing remarkable evolutions, creating illusions
of depth and mass. Like a torrent without banks, or a river of
smoke, they cut figures of eight over a whole sky's quarter,
break up into platoons, regroup. One cannot conceive the
object of this tattoo, of these tight-curved maneuvers.

If you observe your own reactions to such acts of animals,
you may catch yourself being somewhat naïve. You may

surprise yourself interpreting them as though they were human, reading into them plans, reasonings, established conventions. How do otherwise?

One day in Normandy, in the heights of great trees gently plied by the wind, I saw proposed, agreed, and celebrated, a marriage of crows. One really cannot otherwise describe that furiously animated scene in the air. There were two families, future in-laws, the couple, cousins, and aunts. The whole pack of them cawed and gabbled and protested and contradicted; they tore the air to shreds with it. On occasion a party would flap off and go into committee in the blue, then spiral down on to the continuing comedy of the betrothals. Eventually all details seemed to be settled; and the young couple promptly took off amidst the most horrible vociferations, which in our language would have been felicitations, counsels, tender farewells, last blessings and all that apparatus of words-for-the-road which we employ on mighty occasions, for the benefit of those who depart for a while or for ever.

WAKING

On waking: three, four fires of ideas wink into flames at widely dispersed points in the great plain of the mind.

One does not know which to run to.

PSALM T

Of all, the most skeptical
Is Time,
Who out of a No makes Yes,
Who out of a hate makes love,
Of a loving a hating.
And if the river will not turn and ascend to the source,
Or the apple rebound to the twig and remarry its branch,
It is only because you lack the patience to believe they will.

TEARS

I

By a face and by a voice. Life said: I am sad, therefore I weep.
And Music said: I weep, and therefore I am sad.

II

Tears of various ranks. Tears arise from affliction, from impotence, from humiliation, always from a lack.

But some of them, of a divine species, are born of the lack of strength in the soul to support some divine object, to match oneself up to it, to drain its essence.

A story, a mime, a play, can make you weep by their imitations of the sorrows of life.

But if a piece of architecture, which visually resembles nothing human (or indeed any other harmony so exact that it harrows us like a dissonance), carries you to the edge of tears, this upsurge that you feel willed from your inscrutable deeps is of infinite price, for it teaches you that you can be touched by objects wholly indifferent and profitless to your person, your history, your interests, and all the affairs and circumstances that circumscribe you as a mortal.

Poems in the Rough

for Victoria Ocampo

Poems in the Rough

MEDITATION BEFORE THOUGHT

I

IS THERE purer expectation, more detached from the world, emancipated from the self—and at the same time a completer self-possession—than I find at the day's threshold, in that first moment of proposal, of unity of my powers, when the sole desire of the mind (desire preceding all thought) is to steal a march on thought and be the love in what loves?

The soul rejoices in its uncluttered light. Its silence is the sum of all its speech: the sum of all its powers is its repose. It feels withdrawn from names and forms alike. As yet no figuration alters or constrains it. The least act of judgment would spot its perfection.

My body being at rest, I know of nothing except the *potential*. My waiting is a self-sufficient delight: it infers, while it defers, all possible conception.

How marvelous that a universal instant should erect itself in the frame of a man, and that the life of an individual should breathe forth its little puff of eternity!

Is it not in such unmoored states that men have invented the most mysterious and audacious words of their language?

O moment, Time's diamond...I am all trifles and wretched cares outside your gate.

On the summit of being I breathe an indefinable force like the force latent in the air before a storm. I sense the impending.... I do not know what is to follow: but I know what is happening: *to see what exists as purely possible; to reduce what is seen to the purely visible—this is the deepest work.*

II

Ah, consciousness, forever and forever demanding events! No sooner you are, than you are to be filled.

Always you prefer hazard to the void, chaos to nothing.

You are made for all things, and you make yourself anything in your endless metamorphosis.

And, whatever monster you create, you do not want to have looked on him in vain.

Irresistibly also you divide yourself, and cling to one of your parts: some one phantom will drive out the rest; some one word will most prevail; some one idea will spill over its station and endure beyond its instant. Why?—Farewell.

III

The instinct to devour, drain dry, sum up, to express once and for all, be done with, wholly digest, things, times, and dreams; to ruin all by anticipation, seeking thereby some thing other than things, times, and dreams: this is the extravagant mysterious instinct of the intelligence.

The one word World sufficiently proves it.

As always it is Caracalla asking for just one head to cut off.

Laborious nihilism, that reckons nothing well demolished

that has not first been fathomed; and yet its power of *de*struction extends precisely so far and no further than its ability to comprehend *con*struction. A nihilism bizarrely constructive. . . . But it is a case of refusing what one can do— but that capacity has first to be acquired and proved.

MOTIFS OR MOMENTS

W HAT more noble than the immobility of the leaves of the shrub, at calm dawn, when they seem listening to the hymn of light of the rising Sun?

He unfolds the shadows, and the first form of forms is born of his tender power.

His work will become hard and intolerably clear-cut. But now he is still between the rose and gold.

O plant, tree, radial repetition,
You branch on your branching by seasons and by
   shoots,
By rote you repeat your motif exactly
At every landing of every flight
Of your growing stairs: you repeat your essence.
By heart in the seed, it is yourself you make there;
And around yourself it is yourself you cast
From time to time in throws of chance—
   in such numbers
You eliminate your similitudes.

I am the foam that scales the rock, is dashed, falls back,
   a mile away.
My "soul" is "there." "There" is a focus

Where gather, blend, and take on due existence
The forces of shape and of movement that the
Images of that foam excite "in me."
I endow distance, depth, attack, rhythm, duration...
    there, where I am and am not. . . .

This sensation of being hotter than one is.
One wants to strip oneself off like an eider down.
One pities the poor frame,
The hands, the new weight. . . .
Soft would be the lips upon the eyelids,
As the rain closes the flowers,
Cool would be the fingers dispersing
The clouds that blow up each minute
On the brow, on the soul.
Deliciously cool the great pure arms for the acts of
    angels;
Let them enfold the thinking, the burning,
Let them wall about
The Head with the shut eyes, the eyes hidden. . . .
Ah! . . . within the fold of life and the cool cradling flesh
    it desires,
        waits, hopes, creates
A mouth come out of the darkness
Upon it tender and strong. . . .

IN THE SUN

In the sun on my bed after the water,
In the sun and the sun's huge sea-reflection
Below my window and
In the reflections and the reflected reflections
Of the sun and of the sea-suns
In the mirrors after
The bath, the coffee, the cerebrations,
Naked in the sun on my bed flooded with light,
   Naked, alone, mad,
    Myself!

TO LIFE

Bitter as you know how to be—O Life
Bitter and sweet as you know how to be!
Bitter and sweet and heavy as you know how to be,
   O Life
Bitter and sweet and heavy and light and long and
   short as you know how to be, O Life:
As it is only tears that
Can judge, balance, pay for your goods,
So it is only laughter that can truly respond to your ills.

AT THE END

As the great ship is holed and slowly founders with all its stores, its engines, lights, and instruments....

So into the night and the deeps of the self the mind goes down to sleep with all its equipment and potential.

Sleep is more to be respected than death.

FIFTY YEARS AGO

This bird pecks into the dying night with its little sharp cries.... It recalls something.... Resolving into a certain blueness of sky around two or three pricks of stars about to go out.... I make it a memory of my military service. These stars, these *same* cries from over the parade ground, I think of the melancholy, of the Sibyl that they were to me. They were heavy with a meaning that I could not decipher, with the future.... That future has become the past: I know now what was in those presentiments.

DAWN

I

By nothing am I moved more than by summer dawn.

This peacefulness of cool blue painted upon gold, gold and night, gold upon night. This nervous modesty that the sun begins to draw forth out of sleep. There is an instant at which the night is as if visible in the light, just as to the waking mind birth, nonexistence, dreams, are visible in the instant of its first lucidity. Nakedness of the night caught still half-dressed. How strangely gentle is the substance of the sky! One senses to one's very depths this divine freshness, that will be heat quite soon.

One feels the lassitude preceding work, the sadness of re-assuming one's body, older by a day; and hope, and the simplicity of living—its promise, the vanity of its promise. All these mingled (painted as in a primitive picture depicting various acts of the same person all occurring together) upon the purity and the calm. All our poor life in a crystal. There is too that melancholy laziness that precedes great deeds or even the possibility of them. A shyness of entering the day, shiver of first foot in the sea. A golden sadness, a god's. Quiet despair at the cessation of belief in love, in hope.

Before all things. Dumb invocation of what will come, of what may come.

Salutation of the angel announcing that one has conceived and is big with a new day. The Divide.

II

One greets the arrival of activity with a yawn. The body stretches, turns and returns, seeking a torsion and a tension by which to recognize its place within itself, its state of readiness, and to chase away the stalking slumbers.

It is a question of reoccupying the whole, of mopping up the inertias and local resistances.

The mind too leafs itself through—its problems, its dis-quiets, its appointments at all levels. Little by little God disappears behind business matters, under memories, amongst the throng of . . . fact.

PSALM BEFORE THE BEAST

The more I regard you, BEAST, the more I become MAN
And MIND. . . .
You become ever more strange.
Mind knows only the things that are of mind.

In vain by mind I hunt you,
In vain by mind set snares
Baited with gifts of mind:
Origin, purpose, order, principle, cause.

(Or chance even, and all the time that needs;)
O LIFE,
The more I think, the less to thought you yield,
And the least small creature is pleased

To be, to cease, to be again
Quite otherwise than is a thought. . . .
. . . To die, not less than to be born,
Eludes all thought.

Love, death, are not for Mind
That eating amazes, sleeping shames.
My face is a stranger
And the contemplation of my hands,

Their system of forces, obedience, and the arbitrary
Number of their fingers,
Mine and not mine,
Remain unanswered.

68

Not by thought could one divine
His members' roll call or his body's form:
And yet through them alone I know
The Other. . . .

SONG OF THE MASTER NOTION

I

Come! Up! Arise! Hear me!
Hear me! Awake, break chains, be!
Leave shadows, limbos, boundless places, O you far
   absent in the dominion of the unmoving
Pluck yourself out of peace, of night, emerge,
Spread wide your elbows, your wrists, fingers! Stretch!
   Yawn!
Up! Up! Harden, showing your strength! Clench
   teeth,
Remake your statue, climb to its height—quick, foot
   to the plinth!
And let your eyes be a crown of eyes that are clearest.
Be a king! Compose your gaze. Know yourself wholly
The tool of beginning day, of the act that heeds you.
I,
It is I who call you, I who without you can nothing.
I, the Idea,
I who with you can all,
Having been of your darkness and of your composition,
Having been diffuse, near, far (like a drop of wine in a
   vat of sweet water)
In what you were made of.

Aid me! Be flesh, be skeleton,
My form, my eyes, my tongue, my arches.
Be, that I be! Be to be!
Obey, that I be the command you utter!
It is mine, your voice; it is my will you single out.
And what "you" will is... ME! Your Idea!

II

At first I was not. Later, among your thoughts
Born one of many. Innate, inchoate.
But now you are no more yourself wholly;
Yourself, your life, your blood, your fears, your hours,
Your speaking,
Are creatures of the lucky hap, my destiny.
Alone I am the one sole notion shaped
To what you are, and you
Alone my man.
You are my winning streak, and I
The one throw you lost, immortal, unprecedented.
I occurred like a chance in the flux of your mind:
But other hazards and another face of things
Have bound you mine.
To horse! To the chase! In pursuit of what gives you
    life.
You will take me for you, you will think me yourself,
Only over a hidden stone will you stumble....
What I will your eyes will see.
Your common sense will be uncommonly surprised,
Lighting on routes you will not think sane.
Your speech will astound you. Yourself you will run to
    earth,

By achieving your own impossibility.
Your own perspicacity you will not comprehend,
For your own clairvoyance and for your own power
Making apologies, ashamed
Such winnings to have won.
Your humility will mumble that miracles have begun. . . .

III

But all the same what a miracle for me,
Your wretched frame, its paltry person
With his hobbling health,
Self-exacerbated nerves, just what I needed !
What a miracle that made me ! O Human, my condition,
Sole chance
That so many have never had ! in your structure,
In your substance, I have found the hour,
The being, the hour of being, the being of the hour !
The configurations of your memories, with the kind of
    day it was,
How you slept, spent your leisure, your fads and
    fancies—
In your weaknesses I have found my support,
My possibility in your ignorances,
My opportunity in your repulsions. . . .
Now we are one another's, inextricable,
In love !
You are my *Madman-for-my-sake: YOUR IDEA.*

Moments

Moments

THE TEST

I THOUGHT one day of a simple and immediate method of discovering whether a given person has a gift for "mathematics."

It takes some seven or eight seconds, of which six are employed on the question, which is:

"*If Peter resembles Paul, and Paul resembles James, does James resemble Peter?*"

If the subject appears to reflect, the verdict is against him. But if he says "Yes," instantly, without considering the matter, this absolute and unhesitating response "qualifies" him as a student of pure science.

But ill luck would have it that I thought I would test my test and, meeting with one of the best mathematicians of the day, I put the query to him. He began to cogitate at length. . . .

OF COLORS

I

BLACK. "Pessimists of the pen": they seek a "beautiful black," as a painter would say.

Pascal has "beautiful blacks" which he sought out, and to my mind he was all too successful in finding them.

The magnificent "blacks" of the Church, set off by silver and gold.

Organs, vaultings, Latin: *In saecula saeculorum*. . . . Pomps, incense, tapers, heights of deepest shade. . . .

"Pure black," mighty color of the utterly alone; fullness of nothingness. The perfection of *non est*.

II

RED. "Red" is the color of the matter of life.

The red blush of shame announces the rising of the sun of shamelessness within.

A blusher knows a little more than he should.

Blood in the cheeks rudely upsets the arrangement of pursed lips and lowered eyelids, confronting, confounding, the very soul. Its spreading scarlet testifies to the knowledge of Good and Evil.

III

The color of a thing is that one which, out of all the colors, it repels and cannot assimilate. High heaven refuses blue, returning azure to the retina. All summer long the leaves hold in the red. Charcoal gobbles all.

To our senses things offer only their rejections. We know them by their refuse. Perfume is what the flowers throw away.

Perhaps we only know other people by what they eliminate, by what their substance will not accept. If you are good, it is because you retain your evil. If you blaze, hurling off sparkles and lightnings, your sorrow, gloom, and stupidity keep house within you. They are more you, more yours, than your brilliance. Your genius is everything you are not. Your best deeds are those most foreign to you.

MYTHOLOGY

The man who thinks struggles to ferry, to the bank of things from the bank of shadows, such fragments of dream as have some form by which to grasp them—some likeliness or usefulness.

The dream-laden ship founders on the reefs of waking. Crusoe strives to carry back something of value from it on to the beach. Desperate effort.

Nourishment, a necessity: but the food containing it is in part useful, in part not. It sloughs its taste off on the palate.

Taste *veneers* the surface of your food, your mouthful of wine is adorned with bouquet, engendering dreams, profundity.

The living feeling Creature imposes upon things, insisting that they be other things—demanding of them more than their own being and their own substance. He demands of them the accidental.

The world of sound is unlike that of colors, it is not dominated, indeed created, by a single, fabulously powerful sound; there is no *sun of the world of noises*.

THE UNIVERSE

... They were talking about the universe. They calculated its radius, its extension.... I asked them what they meant by the word. I could get nothing sensible out of them. One of them said to me: "It is a sphere outside which there is nothing...." I asked him:

"Would you put pain *in* the universe?"

What more assuredly localized than that?

I said to him also:

"You are going to say something in answer to me. You do not yet know what. Where would you place this answer, of whose existence we are both convinced, in your sphere—outside which there is nothing?"

A CHARITABLE ATTENTION

What a number of things you have not even *seen*, in this street you travel six times daily, in this room where you spend so many hours a day ! Look at the angle between those planes of bookcase and window. Always visible, in vain it has long cried for vision, to be somehow rescued—and you must *save* it—afford it what your arrested sensibility has until now derivatively lavished upon the paltriest sublime prospect, sunset, storm at sea, museum exhibit, or whatever. All that looking is ready-made. But spare something for this poor wretch of a corner, this workaday hour and surroundings, and you will be repaid a hundredfold.

IN THE BEGINNING WAS THE FABLE

Unavoidably.

For *what was* is mind, and its properties are of the mind only.

So, if you consider the reascent to the "beginning," you can conceive of it only as a shedding, item by item, pace by pace, of all that you can infer from experience—or guess, rather, from such increasingly infrequent evidences as still continue to present themselves. And in order to reconstruct for yourself these tableaux as they grow ever more distant, you must resort to filling them out with an ever greater proportion of characters, actions, and scenery, of your own invention.

In the end, there is nothing there that is not *yours*. It is all *you*: pure fable.

THE ASTONISHED ANGEL

The angel was astonished to hear the *laughter* of men.

They explained to him, as they best could, the nature of it.

So he inquired why men did not laugh at *everything* and all the time; or alternatively, did not forgo laughter altogether.

"For, if I understand it rightly," he said, "one must laugh at everything or nothing."

EPIGRAM

Meditation, you are only a word.
Sensitive as a flame to breath,
The mind is blown upon from every direction,
And this must be so,
Otherwise, from the Roman blade
Thinking Archimedes will not shield himself.

ANIMALITIES

I

If children play at tag, the one who is chased will often think to take refuge behind some obstacle such as a big tree or a fixed circular table, and keep running round it at an opposite diameter from that of his pursuer—who will never catch him.

Well, this idea never strikes a hunted animal (?).

The ruses of certain game. It would be interesting to try to trace out the limits of the ideas that can be invented by animals.

II

The whole dog is in his gaze. He throws himself at me with the same devoted leap of his eyes as of his body. He is undivided.

III

Lions have something of narrow surly men about them, a look not found in other animals. Tigers have none of it.

IV

There are animals whose destiny is to follow, nose to ground, the thread of a sort of thought.

This thread is spun of ravelings of smells and snippets of sight, held together only by expectation and a simple trafficking in *yes* and *no*, as they dumbly succeed one another all the way.

This thread is unwound from a reel of walking, of jog trot, itself susceptible of modulation for every this or that.

Their pace is their time.

This thread of immediate attention—snapped by sleep, it becomes dream.

The thread of waking has a live current. That is to say that *no matter what* event is received, its perception can never *totally* alter the face of things; that is what is meant by waking consciousness.

V

The animals that most disquiet man, their horror pursuing him even into his thoughts—cat, squid, snake, spider ... are those whose shape, gaze, and gait have in them something *psychological*. They work upon the nerves by some indefinably sinister magic, enigmatic aspect, as though they were themselves hideous *private thoughts*. Even dead, even flattened, they frighten or excite a most peculiar uneasiness.

These overmastering antipathies bring to light a mythology, a latent store of fable, in us—a folklore of the nerves, hard to isolate, for its borders seem to melt into those of certain effects of sensibility which, for their part, are purely chemical, extrapsychic. Such as gnashing or setting on edge of teeth when faced with the insurmountable; or certain compulsive imitations, ticklishness—all things that provoke unbearable *defense mechanisms (and it is these mechanisms, and not their causes, which are painful)*.

This is a most obscure and most important world—the apparent danger falls absurdly short of the reactions it provokes—and it is these reactions that constitute the real danger.

VI

Animals' gaze.

This gaze of dog, cat, fish conveys to me the notion of a point of view, and of being-viewed-by, and consequently of a private corner, a reserve or self-containment, a chapel that excludes the things that I know and contains only things that I do not.

I do not know of what I am the symbol in that corner. There is a mode of knowing me there. And I am forced to regard myself as a word of whose meaning I am ignorant in an animal system of ideas.

The gaze of creature at creature is the strangest of encounters. To exchange contemplations. This convergence, mutual alignment, virtually double negation!

A sees B who sees A.

B sees A who sees B.

The prodigy of this gaze-in-gaze!

Look at each other a long time without laughing! How

tolerate even a little while to be inscribed one within the other—for the moment of a contradiction?

VII

The animal in fury, in frenzy, wielding his head, his limbs, his jaws, by means of leapings, hurlings, *vis viva*, converts his whole being into the projectile, club, crowbar, battering-ram, and trumpets of a stimulus, which has all these instruments at its disposal.

Broken Stories

Preface

Like everyone else, I sometimes happen to tell myself stories. Or rather, they tell themselves to me. Walking makes them, when it is not hurried and requires no more attention to one's steps than to ensure that they go more or less where one wants to go.

Like fewer people, I also sometimes happen (though rarely) to note down the essence of what has thus come to me. These are "ideas," "subjects" as they are called; it may be two words, a title, a notion. Finally, it also sometimes happens that, reinstalled amongst my papers, I begin to write around what has thus formed independently in my head. I write as though this were the beginning of a book; but I know that this book will never come into being, I realize that I have no conception where it is tending, and that I should be overcome by boredom if I applied myself to directing it to some already determined end. After a few lines or a page I abandon it, having seized in writing no more than whatever had surprised, amused, involved me; and I do not trouble to ask this spontaneous production to extend itself, organize and achieve itself according to the stringent rules of art. At this point, moreover, my morbid sensibility with regard to the arbitrary begins to get in the way. . . .

Every literary work is from moment to moment exposed to the reader's initiative. From moment to moment he can react to his reading by making substitutions which will affect either the detail of the work or its evolution. The background, the narration, and the tone of voice can all be more or less altered, while less or more delicately preserving the effect of the whole. Almost all art consists in persuading the reader to forget his own powers of intervention, in comprehensively forestalling his reactions, in hedging them in through the discipline and perfection of the form. Every story can admit one or more denouements quite other than that which is actually provided; it is much more awkward, by the way, to manipulate at will a well-made poem.

This sensation of multiplication of possibilities, very strong in me, has always turned me away from narration; and I regard the streams that flow from others with the admiration of a man for whom the contemplation and analysis of a glass of water are quite sufficient to absorb his time and curiosity.

Here then is this paradoxical gathering of fragments, of openings, of subjects that offered at various junctures of my life, and which I do not now propose ever to rescue from the fates to which I have abandoned them.

I have added one or two more finished pieces of a poetical nature.

Calypso

HARDLY had CALYPSO appeared to the day's gaze upon the threshold of her sea-cave than every eye was filled with tenderness and every soul with bitterness and burning.

SUBTLY she introduced herself into the visible world, venturing herself measurably, little by little.

By moments and movements exquisitely detailed, she offered part by part her pure flawless body to the sky, until at last she had declared herself wholly to the sun.

YET never did she so advance into the empire of full light that her being was detached entirely from the mystery of the shadows from which she issued.

IT was as though some force at her back restrained her from a complete yielding to the liberties of space, so that for dear life she must remain half the creature of this incomprehensible power, of which her beauty was perhaps no more than a turn of its thought or the incarnation of one of its Ideas, or one of its embarkations upon a desire—a something that was made flesh, launched, in this CALYPSO, at once its organ and its act.

FOR this reason, and because of the cautiousness of her maneuvers, so delicately determined, redetermined, and because of her quivering pearly flesh, she made one fancy her some infinitely sensitive part of the creature of whom, in that case, her cave would have been the inseparable shell.

SHE seemed a dependent part of this shell, the depth of whose inner glooms must be coated with a living substance whose efflorescence all round her, upon the dark rocky edges, decked her in quivering festoons of vanishing ripples, and folds of strangely sensitive tissue that oozed glittering drops.

CALYPSO seemed the natural product of this calyx of wet flesh lolling open about her.

HARDLY had CALYPSO appeared and taken form upon the threshold of her sea-cave than she created love in the fullness of the empty tract. She received it and she returned it with a grace, an energy, a tenderness, a simplicity, that were hers alone.

Yet not without a capriciousness that for her was, no doubt, a law.

FOR eventually she always retired and withdrew herself, for some reason that remained incomprehensible and at a moment that no one could guess. At times this ominous retreat was a stealing away, a dissolving as of a reptile from even the firmest clasp; at times she retracted as suddenly and smartly as a hand that has touched red-hot iron.

And the living mantle of her shell was pursed up about her.

AT once every manner of unimaginable sorrow and evil was let loose under the sky. The whole sea swelled and hurled itself upon the rock, shattering and sacrificing upon it a vast number of its loftiest waves. Shipwrecks were to be seen here and there over the breadth of the whelmed water. The sea boomed and banged frightfully in the submarine cavities of the isle, whose grottoes bellowed appalling blasphemies, obscene railings, or breathed forth sighs that pierced the heart.

Crusoe

CRUSOE had provided all the necessaries and was more or less at leisure in his isle.

He had a good roof over his head; he had made clothes of leaves and feathers, soft shoes, a large light hat. He had led pure water close, right into the shadow of his hut where it prattled like a bird; he was less lonely with this song for companion. Fire served him; he awoke it when he would. From the cabin's rafters hung a multitude of dried smoked fishes; and his great plaited baskets bulged with fat ship biscuits, so hard that they would last forever.

Crusoe forgot his first nakedness and the bitter beginnings of being alone. The time when he went unclothed and had to chase all day after his dinner seemed to him already dim, historical. The era before the shipwreck had become a dream.

He was even surprised now at his own handiwork. The sight of all that he had done amazed him. This happy Crusoe felt himself the heir of a line of beggarly laboring Crusoes rather than the sole strong-willed architect and executant of his own prosperity. It was with the utmost difficulty that he could conceive himself the author of all this that surrounded him, pleasing him and yet dominating him too—for what indeed is odder to a creator than the end product of his work? He has known nothing of it beyond his sketches for parts, fragments, steps to be taken, and his impression of what he has done is quite other than that of the whole and accomplished thing; he has known nothing of its perfection but only of trials, attempts.

A well-found home, stores in plenty, all necessary safeguards taken, inevitably bring leisure. Crusoe amidst his worldly goods became a man again, that is to say a creature of indecision, a being not to be defined in terms of its circumstances alone.

His breathing grew distracted. He hesitated between chimeras: which to pursue? He was threatened with having to invent literature and the arts. The sun seemed needlessly beautiful and it made him sad. He would practically have invented love, had he been less wise and indeed less thoroughly alone.

*

Surveying his mounds of unperishable food, he saw hours of redundancy and of labors saved. A chest of biscuits is a whole month of idleness and life. Those crocks of potted meat, those fiber hampers stuffed with nuts and grain, are a treasury of hoarded repose; a whole easy winter is wafted in their very smell.

In the rank heady odors of the lockers and caskets of his pantry Crusoe snuffed up both the drudgery of his past and the security of his future. It seemed to him that this great heap of his material wealth gave off an odor of indolence, that from it transpired some essence of continuity, as from certain metals a kind of natural heat.

The greatest triumph over matter of man (and of some other species) is to have found out how to carry over to tomorrow the effects and fruits of the labors of today. Only slowly has mankind raised itself upon the platform of what endures. Prevision, provision, little by little they have freed us from the rigors of our animal requirements, from the interminable hand-to-mouth of our needs. We have learned to look around us, away from our natural selves deep-rooted in physical circumstance. Indeed nature itself prompted it, for we carry in ourselves small natural protections against decline. The fat on our limbs permits us to sit out lean times till the good days come again. Memory heaping and building in the dusk of our souls holds itself ever ready to restore to us what the universal flux withdraws from us instant by instant. [Our own industry has copied the model of these reserves; it has made artificial memories.]*

Crusoe had propped against his hearth an old book of logarithms which he had saved from the waters and of which either the flames or hard usage were beginning to devour the pages. These leaves all smothered in tiny figures, so that one would have sworn them marched upon by echelons of ants, affirmed in their simple decimal tongue that our busy species has discovered how to bank truths and to bequeath legacies of the *achieved*. The long pains of someone, his wakeful nights, lay hoarded in these ingenious cypherings: the application and the talents of the few supply the want of them in all the rest.

*

He thought how the Egyptians and others had pushed the instinct to preserve the perishable to the point of claiming to arrest the decomposition of the dead.

* Struck out in the MS.—J.M.

Indeed they, and many peoples with them, had hoped that *souls* might be indestructible too. They had not seen that incorruptibility, immortality, existence apart from time (that is to say, from circumstances) imply meaninglessness, indifference, total isolation—in a word, nonexistence.

*

Provident labor reminds one of certain board-games in which a skillful stroke releases squares and allows new liberties of maneuver. But the definition of a "society" is that it neglects the letters in a man's head in favor of those after his name.

Providence lays up supplies of leisure yet to come.

The accumulation of resource.

We are brought once again to consider that a stretch of time may be in essence a group rather than a series and permit the *exchange of minute for minute* as one will.

*

With regrets he looked back upon the days of fear, of hunger, of the companionship of definite needs.

When he needed love.

*

Amnesia from shock. A knock on the head in the shipwreck robbed his memory in part.

Crusoe lost an area of knowledge, in form irregular and bizarre as an island continent whose contour derives solely from the height of the sea.

Islets of memory, reached dry-shod.

His island.

Tides of slumber, spring or neap.

God mislaid, regained.

Himself bright, dull; and at his least remembering himself
to have once been *more*.

A monologue, of course.

Crusoe makes an audit of his whole estate. His situation.
A balance-sheet. His memories, powers.

Complete works of Crusoe.

*

Crusoe.

Solitude.

The creation of leisure. Capital of reserves.

Vacant time. Decorating this.

Danger of losing his head, of losing his tongue.

Conflict. Tragedy. Memory. Crusoe's prayer.

He calls up crowds, streets, theaters.

Temptation. The thirst for London Bridge.

He writes to imaginary persons, embraces trees, talks to
himself. Gusts of laughter. Little by little ceasing to be himself.

There comes upon him an invincible horror of the sky, sea,
nature.

Forest murmurs.

A naked foot.

Crusoe's psalms.

Isolating set pieces, contrasting, working out.

*

Forest murmurs.

Crusoe among the birds, parakeets, etc. He fancies he
understands their language.

All these birds speak proverbs. They iterate them.

Some original.

Others repeat truths which become false by the mere act of repetition.

*

Crusoe pensive.

(The Castaway's Handbook.)

God and Crusoe—(new Adam)—

Crusoe's temptation.

The footprint in the sand, he believes it is a woman's.

He imagines Another. Man or woman?

Crusoe divided—poem.

Sunset—Sea.

*

"Crusoe pensive"—closed system.

—the moment of reflection.

—the utilization of dreams.

Theory of the exact model. The 3 axes of reference.

Memory.

But from all that he once knew he has retained only what was agreeable to his substance.

*

Crusoe

(1) reconstructs what he has read.

(2) rejects it.

*

Without books, without writing, Crusoe re-creates his intellectual life. All the music that he has heard comes back to him—pieces he never knew he knew ever. His need, his solitude, the emptiness, develop the organ of memory; and it alone sustains him. He wins back books he has read; he notes what he is able, or not able, to regain. His results are highly surprising.

And eventually behold him *developing* upon all this, creating in his turn.

*

This Crusoe must contemplate human affairs and consider them "sub specie intellectus."

Literary squabbles, for example—his method will be explication, the teasing out of the implicit; *what has to be done* to bring about such and such an effect.

Sample: the angry, wounded, riled, jealous, who (to such as will listen) cry out upon the object of their hate or envy, "You will pass, you will be blotted out, because it *has* to be I, because it has to be *I*, who will take the place which now you hold in the opinions of those whose opinions, for that matter, I take to be the vaporings of ghosts"; and such-like follies.

These things are projected upon the screen of Crusoe's solitude.

*

Charming and intelligent men of all nations, beings made for mutual understanding, for the free exchange of thoughts, you are slaves and victims of the most brutal of men, the greediest, the stupidest, the most gullible, of those indeed who neither know nor wish to know the true enemies of humanity (being of their party), and want what beasts want, neither more nor less.

You obey them, you consider them, etc., they give you a guilty conscience. Yet all their strength is simply your own weakness; your sorrows are the fruits of your own credulity.

*

The mind is attached to the body in rather the same way as a man is to the planet.

The planet turns and is part of him, and he is unaware of it.

He knows only his surroundings and immediate possibilities. He is quite unable either to imagine or to perceive relationships and connections far away.

Of the body the mind sees nothing but the body, but knows it not in time. The mystery of memory.

The Earth (weight, mass, light, rotation) maintains existence only within a system (time, action).

The mind has only the most restricted, the incompletest, notion of the body's system, and of that to which the body belongs.

An endless system of dependences.

*

From collections, recollections, he reconstructs his library—and finally creates his art.

Discouragement.

Wishes to end himself, but bethinks himself that it is traditional, too like . . . and cannot even do that.

Friday.

*

The notion that death should be the chief subject of reflection of the living, and their chief care, was born with luxury—with the acquisition of abundance.

Whence this odd question: Among the choice of useless things, which do we give our minds to?

*

Crusoe ends by having created his own island.

I *counter* every tedium, want, irritation, by the vision of a condition in which they could not touch me: hence the image of a golden island where nothing could reach me (nothing of remembrance above all) except what would please.

Or rather, I should *begin* by shutting the whole thing off at once, my island.

But later I see inconveniences in this insular perfection; and I allow in, but only on certain days, at certain hours, some news, friends, books....

It is memory that has furnished my island—malleable memory, pliable to the moment's needs.

Against my boredom I have constructed its precise negation. Then I have added to this negation certain positives, things actively desired: the sea, the south, etc.

From such denying, such desiring, a sort of riddle or enigma has been formed, whose solution is an image that is *exact*.

I could draw this island on the sea.

Observe that this island where *you would be*, you imagine it seen from afar, conical, gilt, pale....

What a mixture!

"Why should a chimera of this sort answer these requirements?"

Requirements? The word is a trifle narrow. *Because*—I have another *response* to such peace, plenitude—an image of bad moments, gloomy forebodings, a hideous chaos....

So there he is, Crusoe, on his cubic island.
Evening falls. The tenderest blue is on the glass

Of the high windows.
Coffee and Tobacco
People the shadows and the Palate.
Tyrannous labor recedes before the dying day
And what she, the other, thinks is a faraway
Intimate murmur which is not the city's.
Alone, Not Alone: Crusoe.

CRUSOE

"Leisure," said Crusoe, "Leisure, daughter of salt, of cooking, of dressings that arrest the proper fates of perishable foods; daughter of smokings, of preservative fumes, of aromatics, spices, of logarithms even—what shall I do with you? What will you do with me? No longer do my desires and hungers color and portion out my days. I dream no more of action, I see no more mirages of roasted prey, and I am free. Is that not to be without form? When we fancy we at last possess ourselves, in fact we fall under the domination of the pettiest things about us. The infinite variety of inessential objects hides from us our own powers. My only law is now my indifference. My mobility paralyzes me. My lightness weighs me down. My security does not fail to trouble me. What am I to do with this wealth of time that I have put by?"

The Story of Hera

EVERY MARK of power was visible in the beauty of Hera. She was a tall woman, statuesque, of noble form and fine proportion. As a human plant she was vigorous and rich in growth. Yet her step was light, and each of her movements precisely controlled. A watchful intelligence lit up her eyes whenever a new idea, her own or another's, amused, annoyed, or astonished her. Her voice was softer than one expected: its shadings belonged rather with the delicacy of her gestures than with the majesty of her body and her classic style of beauty. This happy contrast made her dangerously charming. And there was another contrast between certain properties of her inner nature that revealed themselves in the course of her outward life. This beautiful head dreamed and imagined and told itself all the tales that any woman will who knows herself to be sensitive and seductive: yet common sense and calculation always managed in the end to impose themselves on her thought with such dominion and clarity that they bore down all the forces of her heart, no matter how drawn by the tenderest bonds toward some living being. She would suppose herself truly in love; but she was like those cautious bathers who swim with three limbs only and find a footing again as soon as they feel the bottom fail them—she was conscious of a certain point of self-abandon that she must not pass beyond. Thus her light step firmly and deliberately trod down all those flowers sprung from herself, or all the others that impeded her journey toward a goal. Her voice altered, and her gaze became hard and brilliant with the effect of her arrested notion. She saw what she wished to see, down to its least detail, and there was nothing in the conception or in the execution of any of her plans that she did not visualize with the utmost precision, arguing it over with herself laboriously and minutely. Never was she so distracted as to forget that love is not all.

All this made of her a creature at once splendid and formidable.

Nothing sacred for her. She valued nothing more highly than her will to live as agreeably and richly as she could. All her desires were aimed at the sure and concrete. But, conscious of something second-rate in this, she hid it from herself, building herself a romance of a humble life devoted to an ideal of love and spiritual labor; for she was aware that her consuming passion for luxury, elegance, and a flattering reputation was insufficient substance for that perfection that she desired for her whole being. She loved poetry and was moved by it, even the subtle or exalted. But this fine sensibility was not so dominant in her that she would set an "infinite," that is to say a vital, price upon the passions of the intelligence. They too were for her an adornment of the exterior. Significantly, films were her least dispensable entertainment; she was moved by them—but unmoved by the stupidity and the coarseness of the means. Refined as she was in regard to her dress and her furnishings, she did not perceive that to frequent such spectacles, and to extract pleasure from them, was like clothing oneself and one's apartment in shoddy articles of mass production—which she detested.

By her judgment of carnality she was judged. She inadvertently let slip the observation that the fact of *f...
together was of no importance*—and she actually said it to Gozon himself, to whom it showed her up in a most distressing light, since he was the most irritable and obstinate of beings on this subject. He agreed with her in all cases where love was no more than pleasure. But he found that intimacy *in the act* becomes a sort of secret communion when a holy loving-kindness and a sense of the marriage of souls exalts it, rendering it a means toward the profoundest identification of two beings.

"You are in hell," Gozon told her, perfectly seriously.

The Slave

MEMORIES are lies, and stories are fit only for children. Listeners to tales are more simple-minded than those snakes the charmer induces to sway to the bewitching flute: they obey the word, they surrender to its illusions, they are cold or hot or shuddering or exalted, shieldless before the arms of language. For them, the phrases are real creatures, sentences are events! ... And as for those who take pleasure in doctrines, expecting philosophers to light up the grotto of the soul and the cavern of this world, they are the most infatuated of all.

*

I was a slave, and also the happiest of philosophers. I had been taken at sea, drunk with wind, weariness, and watches; drunk with the void, deaf, my limbs battered all over by the endless pitchings and yawings of the boat, which had not stinted to pass on to me all the rough transports of an interminable tempest. I was picked up and brought ashore. Yet scarcely had I touched dry land than my saviors bound me on the spot for sale. However, the queen of that country, learning the news that I was of Byzantium and a pupil of the pupils of Metrodorus, debated long over me and then reserved me for her private use. She had a little gold chain tied about my neck, that I would habitually suck and gnaw.

Soon I was in some doubt whether I was the creature of her imperial power or of her haughty looks and glittering limbs. I thought no longer of my own country. When the introspective man discovers in the outward world the very object to satisfy his unending contemplation, he and his former life part company with ease. My new days grew and multiplied like thick bushes between my memories and my heart.

This outlandish sovereign never wearied of hearing me. She ordered me to talk about everything. I squatted on my heels, under the dominion of her countenance. Stretched on her couch this woman assumed the long-drawn form of a peninsula that terminated in [the shell-work of]* her marvelously bright and tinted feet. Sometimes, by reason of these delicate extremities, I passed beyond all knowledge of what I was saying. She loved me to lose myself before her in the disputations of demons that I brought surging to my lips. Her dark eyes drank from my babbling mouth; and sometimes suddenly her own mouth fluttered down upon some flower of my discourse. She enjoined me never, upon pain of death, to speak with any save herself alone. The very notion of my past tormented her. She could not contemplate without bitterness that I had lived before I knew her. It was a hateful thought to her that I had once demonstrated the elements of logic to the Amazons,** and the theory of the lyre to the young layabouts of Phocaea. She had me whipped for telling her, with a degree of complacence, something of those epochs in my life. Afterwards she kissed my weals, murmuring: *I shall fasten these stinging pains to your pleasant memories.*

One day when she had given me her usual command to say what I would, silence seized me by the throat. I found

* Added in MS.—J.M.
** Alternative in MS: *to the courtesans of Corinth.*—J.M.

nothing in myself beyond the simple sensation of my own existence. Truths and lies alike were suddenly deaf to the urgent pleadings of my soul. In vain did my inner voice repeat the sesame, the queen's words before the locked doors of my private treasure-cave.... Ah, multifarious knowledges! Ah, endless combinations, puzzles, parables, mysterious recitals whose silk the teller spins spiderlike out of himself, descents into the kingdom of the white cypress and black lake, sleights of heroes, peccadilloes of gods, voyages, drawn morals, subtleties, the totality of all that can be said.... All this razed to nothing!...

What presence so unreliable as that of our intelligence? And how can all its riches evaporate without cause, and all our knowledge plunge without warning into the depths of ourselves?

I had an obstinate vision of a pink house *that I knew to be deserted* and, in the sky over this symbol of my dumbfounding, a headlong flight of cranes. I suffered cruelly at this baffling suspension of my thought: my tongue grew dry; my face was as if exposed to fire.... The queen closed her eyelids in order to observe me within.

There followed a time made purely out of time, a time standing disastrously still, an interval between two seconds that nevertheless dragged on insupportably forever!... And now you shall hear how we finally emerged from this period without exits.

My eyes wandered distractedly, in the pursuit of Idea. They found nowhere, neither upon the walls nor upon the hangings of the royal chamber, the form of man or of animal, nor any shapes that might be recognized, nor anything (no matter what) that bore any resemblance to anything: up, down, to right, to left, all was incommunicable fantasy, dumb antics, sinuations, pure and complex developments, ordered surprises and willing enchainments, embroidered upon the draperies, encrusted into the tiling, painted on the beams, worked or cameoed upon precious stones, etched or illuminated upon everything. . . . All fled any likeness. . . .

"Queen," I cried, "queen! . . . pearl and *primum mobile* of this cell of enchantments and of unspeakable joys,"—and here the brightness of her look encouraged me—"fair sovereign Queen, I no longer know what I knew . . . as a man who has lost his malady and feels no more pain is astonished, and even alarmed. . . .

"But I can feel in myself now a new spirit, pure, a new grace of speech and feeling . . . a new infinite that. . . . "

(*Scholium*)

One day when she gave me her usual command, "Say what you will," I remained silent. For I had come to an end of my histories, and all that I knew had been made known to her. For her I had exhausted all my narrations, developed all my doctrines, revealed the origins of all the gods, the adventures of all the heroes, the illustrious deeds of all famous men. My mind was desert, the hives empty, truths and untruths were alike failed springs, and there was nothing in me beyond this sesame of the queen's words that in vain I repeated before the locked doors of my treasure-cave. I despaired of my daemon. But suddenly I was lit with inner light. How the paths of the mind are. . . .

*

I shall sing the senses.

It is the senses are truth, the senses are purity. For the real object in itself signifies nothing and alludes to nothing. Not to memory, nor to interpretation, nor to reason. But the senses, present sensations, immediate objects, in these lies profundity!

There are no deceptions for the senses: they say what they say, and if they happen to fall into contradiction, if the hand contradicts the eye, each remains honest in its own sector and operation. If you see something painted and if, trying to grasp it, you find nothing but the flat of the canvas, blame the painter, not the senses! And blame yourself for making inferences from one world to another, and for putting your faith in a *thing*!

Queen supreme and lovely, your eyes open again to tell me I am mad. Indulge them, those eyes, for I tell you they are what is profoundest in us. Don't think. Let your eye live its life.

The adornments about you, inviting the philosopher's contemplation, are what the eye, left to its own devices, would conceive for its own good, in order to receive what it gives and to desire what it possesses.

*

But the eye has its own understanding.

One might say that each of our senses has its own mode of understanding; and that it marks its failure to understand by its suffering.

To comprehend is to *discover* what one might have created for oneself; it is to recognize oneself, to find that an external object *is* in fact oneself, for oneself, of oneself.

It is to measure—or to discover the scale of measurement, the terms upon which the object is to be reconstituted.

Our senses were always desiring, but in the dark, what our intelligence failed to expect.

Elisabeth to Rachel

... a distinctly frightening faculty of seeing everything in his life, of seizing it, concentrating, transmuting it, as though by some process of chemical analysis or of digestion, into an essence of contempt, an excrement of his experience, and yet into a force and a celerity of his mind. Our beauty, our graces, our pleasant voices, what does this monster do with them? What the tiger does with the speed and elegance of the antelope: he reduces them to tiger and excrement.

Sometimes he felt pity ... and that was worst of all! For then one felt he hated his pity and that it would be a fuel for his anger, for the reflaring of his fury; that he would despise his compassion and make us pay for it. Take care, my pretty one! And listen to this too: never (if you can!) allow yourself to be examined too closely by that gaze of his—confound his eyes with yours, and the play you make with them. Believe me, our whole magic shuns the being too known. I cannot imagine how angels could have let themselves be seduced by the daughters of men. Blind angels!

Fancy, one day he said to me: "Love is a commerce of juices"! True, he said on another: "My faculty of seeing too much maddens me at times. I hate myself when I feel it at work: for it brutally drags out into the hard light those things whose whole value is to be their shades."

So, I have conceived a violent desire to subdue this Gozon. He says his ancestors number a dragon-killer. I feel within me a very wivern-like spirit, and the will to reduce him to despair gnaws at my heart—it gnaws itself within me.

Rachel

(Emma?
Laura?)

RACHEL
or
SOPHIE
or
HAGAR

Where I was born was where I was born to live, and where I have not lived, but in spirit am carried there by a sort of leap within whenever I am sore at heart, unhappy, weary of being, furious with my private fury, *the fury of being some-one*, gnawed by my very existence, even when enjoyable, turning as it does to haphazard pain: then, *being stabs me through*. So my eyes close, and a window opens with precisely the swiftness of the lids that fall, and I repair to a light in myself that never fails—it is the here and now as it flies. At once appears this almost square window upon the right hand of my thought. Sometimes it is checkered by Venetian blinds; sometimes it has a balcony of prettily wrought iron. A secret thought lurks in the answering shadow where I should be. Or sometimes it rockets like a bird, traversing suddenly the outer fire of day, winging to inspect a distance that is still *I*, then homing again out of that radiance into the closeness of a dark that is *I* too. There is talk in the room, and this answers my eyes—I mean it answers rather to the action of my closed eyes, as they touch and play with a thousand things of possibility: a high lighthouse, ancient roofs, the smokes of chimneys. When the window comes, I am capable of everything, there is no pure folly, pure truth, undertaking, crime, panic flight even, that is beyond my powers. Nothing arrests the march of my thought; I go to its hardest limits.

*

At such times I seem to myself an island, or a being in a state of desperation; one that lives by the knife: I seem to myself a tower of a woman, wholly beset by pitiless enemies from whom she draws a strength that is infinite and implacable: These are strengths no strength can conquer. In the hospital I have seen a tiny madwoman knock down six strong men. I have read in the gospels of the woman with the issue of blood, and have thought that it was a virtue such as is my virtue that went out then from the being of Christ—to His astonishment (and that He *could* be astonished is even more astonishing ! . . .). And then my heart fails, the window fades, and once again I am weak and absolutely charming to everybody. When love came, this too was an alien force; and when I inspired it, I too felt that I was inspiring it by way of some virtue that went out of me, and that I never knew I possessed. A certain fragrance of flowers brings the window, and love with it.

That day, the window was good, gilded with morning. Then simultaneously I was invaded by one odor of coal, and another of sweet basil (which I detest). For it comes to me out of childhood, an aroma bringing with it unhappiness.

Apparently I am possessed of a will and a weakness whose mixture is incomprehensible to all, their oppositeness baffles everyone. It is an intoxicating mixture. I can seduce pretty well anyone I wish. But the whole matter is unclear to me. I am as I am, I argue in my favor, but I don't at all like me. I like those beings I should like to be, and those I should like to understand. Death can take the rest for all I care and. . . .

*

What is called *Love* has played in my life the part which, in other more remarkable and no doubt profound lives, is taken by certain rare and secret happenings, revelations, apparitions, coincidences, unexpected illuminations. . . . These are like very serious accidents along the road of life; they have extraordinary consequences that leave us quite other than we were, having evoked from us the most surprising reactions—which would have remained always unknown, or even unimaginable, had not such and such a collision or such and such an hour, more irruptive than all its fellows, thrown us out of the straight way.

Thereafter relations between oneself and one's self are quite altered, and this may occur at any time.

*

But I was wrong to use that word *Love*. It is merely odious to me. It is an omnium-gatherum: a need, a sport—an animal dance—a terrible sickness snarling up wits and nerves—an idolatry complete with rites, dogmas, sacrifices, or a sort of sleepwalking with tumblings off roofs into roads. . . .

No, too convenient a word by half. And then too . . . *it makes all alike*. I never could bear the sensation of singing what has already been hummed to death by everybody. That is why I hate life, nature, memory. . . . And all that. It is a sort of private madness. I know it. And so I have always tried to avoid being *known by heart*.

*

This LOVE business presents itself to my intelligence in a sufficiently odd form. Once I had got a rough idea of what it was all about, my whole knowledge seemed reduced, crystallized, to two questions—which indeed may perhaps be only one? . . .

What can one make of ANOTHER?

What can one make with ANOTHER?

Thus for me this famous LOVE business has assumed the features of an OTHERS business—a single, though particularly important, aspect of the whole OTHERS business in general.

I have been led to this idea by certain experiences.

These acts are so strange, so utterly removed from anything one could have visualized, so little natural in fact, that I am hard put to understand how *animals* ever manage to rediscover them, reinvent them. They are neither simple nor obvious nor even very easy. The ancients were well aware of this. I have read *Daphnis and Chloe*.

But nothing is less simple than nature.

RACHEL

OR

HAGAR

. . . " And I realize that I am looking for a religion which does not sell heaven but gives it. HEAVEN, FREE! I have always been disgusted by trade. I give willingly, I receive joyfully; but no bargaining.

115

"But the Father, the other day, remarked: 'Heaven is within you.' This strange little phrase lay uneasily upon my mind: it appeared to be ferreting there for a precise meaning; and this quest for precision led me into wicked thoughts. . . ."

To feel that within oneself one carries, at the mercy of one's actions—which are themselves at the beck of a moment, a look, a random notion, a glass of champagne, a tone of voice, a nothing, a sense of vacuum above all: to feel that within oneself one carries the violent power of one's personality at its most extreme. . . .

And this so near, so far. . . . Does one ever know?

And this, so stupid, so dirty, so sweet, so alive—so sad too. . . .

Is one ever sure that one's food is not a poison?

How does it come about that all is altered at a blow, and the forces and the frailties of one's body combine to pull one down to drown?

Oh those small hours ! . . .

"Ah, Father, you must not go on reiterating like that that God is love and that heaven is within us.

"Ah, Father, I know one thing only: He is the stronger. That's what He is for me, God: He is the one who in the end is always the stronger. . . . And—excuse me, forgive me, understand me—that's the long and the short. If I understand the dogmas aright, we are, and necessarily, in a condition of perpetual struggle against Him. Sometimes we pick up a point here and there, but He always wins the rubber."

And the Father said to me: "No, my daughter, He does not win: if you lose your self, then all the world loses, both He and you alike."

"But, Father, what has He to lose? Is there loss for Perfection?"

"He loses the love that He bore toward you. His stake in your soul."

"And that is Hell?"

"Yes, my daughter."

"But . . . to cause God a loss is, after all, something."

The Island of Xiphos

I AM at present in Firgo. It is an island. Or rather, it was an island but today it is joined to the mainland by two tongues of fine sand which year by year are broadening more and more into beaches. The peak of this island is some six hundred feet above the sea and from its topmost rock one sees, or rather used to see, or perhaps used to think one saw, further land upon the south horizon. Actually, those who said they had seen it added that they had never seen it again. They called it XIPHOS, and according to them it was the last remaining fragment of the world that preceded ours. They spoke (but in bated breath) of a thousand marvels in it —marvels such that the chief end of our modern human intellect should be (if there were in existence minds able to tackle it !) to sift out the true from the false in these whispered legends, and with the utmost application to reconstruct the knowledge, the powers, and the desires of those who once lived there. They say they knew a thousand thousand times more than we, or knew something altogether different, and for that reason I wonder if they are really to be called Men. They would refuse us the name, no doubt; so perhaps we should speak of them as *angels* or as *demi-gods*. Our relative situation is barely analogous to that which subsisted between Europeans and the most primitive savages encountered in exploration.

After all why should not the irradiated generative surface of the earth have brought to being species as superior to man as he is to the other mammals?

Gozon remarked in good faith: "They possessed every sort of morality, and I possess every sort of morality. I am wicked and I am virtuous and both to excess. There is no one more impious or more devout than I feel myself to be. Truly, *my nature defies definition*. It pushes me to extremes— contradictory ones! So that I feel that I am quite literally nothing. Perhaps I am some lone survivor from that era in which the sexes were not yet separate, nor was science yet divorced from art, nor strength from grace, nor freedom from the knowledge of law, nor even vice from virtue? A whole species possessing the protean properties of mind. Their god was like no other. Their dreams were part of their waking, and their waking was busy about more dreams, that were to react upon it at their next waking; or rather to develop in total freedom new combinations, new and rare simultaneities of sensation."

The most famous of our chess players, those who play ten games blindfold at once, and win them; our greatest mathematical prodigies: compared with most of those islanders they would be no more than children counting on their fingers.

It appears that their senses were as superior to ours in their powers of analysis as in their powers of combination. They say some of them had never heard two sounds that were identical: they distinguished two notes of the same pitch sounded upon the same instrument under the same conditions. . . .

Love. There are only two things the living have to do: to feed and breed. All else is inconsequence, meaningless, luxury, perversion, distraction.

THE ISLAND OF XIPHOS

. . . There stood in a little square, surrounded by houses with curious ornaments, of fresh or of faded gilt, a pedestal bearing a woman of flawless beauty, clean-cut as a statue, in a noble pose. Several times a day she was to be heard speaking or declaiming poetry at length. Then she would begin to sing. There was so perfect and so elemental a consonance between the tone, the inflections of her voice, and the successive positions of her body answering from head to ankles to every variation in her breath, that one stood arrested in submission to the power of Purity.

Her function was to fix the language of the country and to sound, as a clock sounds true hours, the most desirable accent and the most elegant syntax of that tongue.

On certain days she would speak the truth to whoever wished to hear it; and she spoke it with so lucid a diction, so searching a cadence, so bewitching a harmony between the expression of her face and the perfection of her speech, and above all with so plenary a concord of her entire body whose least parts in their slightest tensing or most delicate ripple of muscle evidenced that nothing was withheld, no lies whispered aside, that in general everyone was too frightened to question her. It seems that the whole body is incapable of maintaining a lie, and that is why Truth is represented naked. However, I was informed that some persons had protested against using so beautiful a woman so, alleging that Truth is far more often ugly, indeed may be the hideous truth. But no account was taken of this.

She held the rank of priestess. Whether a virgin, is uncertain. Daughter of whom and of whom? I have no idea.

Toward sunset she fell upon her knees. . . .

Of the Temples and Sanctuaries of Xiphos

I

There was in Xiphos, inland, on a mountain, a temple apparently older than the island itself, being ingeniously constructed from prismatic blocks of a black stone not local to it, which were riveted together with an unknown metal. And in it was preserved a head with closed eyes, that spoke. And the head was within the temple, but within the head was the universe. They broke it open and . . . crystal dice of which one is now in Rome, the other in. . . .

Oracles, pronouncements, issued out of it. It wrought justice by yea and nay and delivered counsel upon everything. An inscription upon it read: *I have no heart.*

(Dialogues of X with the head.)

Here follow some of the aphorisms of this prodigy, and some of its remarkable consequences.

II

And there was also a grotto scooped out of the mountain by some unknown hand and whose entrance, facing the sea, was shaped to symbolize woman. [Only men would enter it, anointed with unguents, the face veiled.]* There, at the brim of the cavern, stood a sort of isolated column, erected in the shadow's cool—yet it was itself always almost red-hot. Whoever touched this fetish was turned into a bull.... Groups of girls hung about outside for those who came forth. Etc....

III

And there was also a Book, in itself incomprehensible; but whoever gazed at it while thinking of the thing he wished to know, felt he could read it.

A fountain? A tree?

Xiphos where all is symbol—(Dreams)—

All sign—how to make that understood? Nothing without significance, *thus all* commutable.

The head frequently remarked, "Cogito, non sum." A certain Ælianus of Colophon held a conversation with it, even a kind of dispute. This the head countered by supplying all the alternative answers possible, insinuating thus its disdain for truth. Then it proceeded to insults.

The animals there were those we find in fable. They looked men straight in the eyes, harming them in no way but intimidating them strangely. Men perceived in them a quite other order of perception and at once felt themselves to be no more than one species among many, stripped of all pretension to universal knowledge. Was it from this came that legend of looks that turn to stone? The truth goes deeper still, and is that....

* In the margin of the MS.—J.M.

Island of Xiphos (or the place
of Wicked thoughts)

... At Xiphos there was a god who rejected not merely prayers but even those *inward* posturings that other gods appear to exact from their creatures. "With the most part of your pretended believers," he would say to the other gods, "what they call their 'faith' is a constriction, a craning of the neck, a struggle painful to see, which may become a mere nervous tic; it is something contagious, imitative, born of fear, even of boredom sometimes, and only too often the result of a crude attempt to deceive you. They say to you what they have been taught to say and do not and could not think, but are substituting speech for thought.... And what they say to you is pointless. Do they imagine they have something to teach you?

"But I," he added, "I am the god of those who resist me in so far as I am and desire me in so far as I am not. *Ah!*, they say, *if only there were a god!* They are not afraid to deny or remain ignorant of such things as they can neither see, nor conceive; or to reduce whatever is offered to them as 'holy,' or which they feel to be such, to its true status as a product of their own nature—a product often full of beauty or of power but which can never be of a different substance and modality from the other constructs of their intelligence. In such an attitude there is something I esteem, which is their attempt to abstain from creating a creator and universal lord, and so on."

*

(The philosophers.) One who took time *literally* as a Heraclitean flux, and set himself to scientifically investigate the hydraulics of the events and states of that river, attempting to deduce the equations of flow, of pressures, of eddies—of effects of rams.

This approach, applied to impressions, ideas, sensations, actions and reactions of *every sort*—as though to floats—should yield singular principles and laws.

Effects of relative motions.

How to explain our impercipience of this flux?

Flux as *substance* (in fact, an unperceived *sense-datum* because INVARIABLE. Cf. radio-telegraphy, the "carrier-wave").

And *flux* as *alteration*—the sensed fluctuations of the "modulating-wave"—

Perhaps it is from the interference-beats set up by these two waves, these two aspects of flux, when their ratio is consonant, that we derive our sense of rhythms?

*

Crystal song of the statue of Memnon.

A—when the sun first shows and the ray strikes.

B—when the sun leaps up—

I, washed in dew—at first I murmur, faintest cries, then sing —Substance: noise of cracking—Source: sun, on eyes that are blind—and finally the radiance has dried the dew.

I sparkle dumb—

*

...He recited to us one or two poems of his own composition.

Then he showed us the texts of some that had been collected from the Sacred Mouth (as they call the mouth of the Speaking Head).

However, the script was unknown to us. Then he explained to us that the value of a poem is the same as the number of senses that it can bear, and that these possessed twelve primary meanings, from which a dozen more could be inferred.

Compare convex polygons, their faces cut to form stars.

*

Marriage in Xiphos

... Young marriageable men were shown, one by one, a company of young girls who did not know they were under observation and of whom each wore some token or hair style that would distinguish her from the others.

They said which they preferred, and this was noted.

The same experiment was tried with each girl selecting from among the boys. Comparing their choices yielded various results.

The Temple of Fear

Fear, essential—the basis of every society.

There is no society of heroes. However, a very early attempt at Xiphos.

*

The severed Head sees things as they are, pure Present, meaningless, no top nor bottom, faceless, without pattern.

But a diversity.

And when the lag in the retina's reactions increases. ...

No answers—eternally suspended judgment—

For all *judgment is hasty*.

Speaks too soon, puts an end to what is not—never—finished.

No *transition*.
neither past nor future—
no numbers.

*

In the island of Xiphos there was a district in which were confined all those suffering from the disease called *Anastrophe*. After performing any action its victims immediately performed its opposite—or else its simulacrum: a thing terrible to be seen rather than merely absurd. Other lunatics repeated each action many times over.

—There was a sort of house of *Egophobes*, where those lived who never spoke of themselves. The words *I* and *Me* were never heard there.

The Beggars

Oh yes, they had beggars! Some begged for love. Others for esteem. Others for glory. And they looked down upon such as demanded food or money. Some put out their hands for an idea, God bless you kind sir, or a good couplet—or a style that could be called "original."

*

The Shops

The poet's shop—the mathematician's, etc.
  You can see them at work, that's the point.
  Streets of a fantastic Paris—names of the streets—

"Taste and compare"—words worthy of a Gospel.
  Work well and let them talk.
  The Mantuan style of verse is practiced here.

The poet's shop—a little copper lyre hanging, a parrot speaking in verse (says Latin verses), blackbirds, a flavor of magic, Hoffmannesque.

The muse, seated. Rush chair.

His apprentices—Socrates' Daemon Street.

*

The Mutes.

"All that issues from man is impure" was their view, and so they kept as silent as possible.

They were bursting with love and ideas bottled up inside the precincts of their superstition against all outflowing.

*

The restorer's philosophy.

"Moral" tale, or prose poem with a refrain.

The restorer of pottery, porcelain, marble, alabaster.... Such beautiful words. And then one discovers this man seated upon the steps of the church. He lists his pleasures—one cannot stop listening.

Accident assumed. Philosophy of the broken vase—game of Patience.

*

Anecdote. A strange torture:

The king ordained ("I condemn you to death, but only in so far as you are Xios, and not in so far as you are You") that Xios should be taken into quite another part of the country. His name to be changed, his features cunningly altered. His new neighbors to be obliged to attribute to him a past, a family, abilities, altogether different from his own.

If he mentioned anything of his former life, they would deny it, tell him he was mad, etc....

They had a family all ready for him, a wife and children who said they were his.

In a word everything assured him that he was who he was not.

*

The Forbidden Museum of Xiphos

The painted tableaux in the style of Philostrates of Athens—or in other words the *Neocosmos*. . . .

"Knowledge being sacrificed by Science" was the subject of the principal fresco of the period.

"Suicides and Paradoxes"—(find adjectives). . . .

"Europe expiring *in media insanitate* !"

"Faith devouring her Children" (Justice, Truth, etc.).

"The Twilight of the Infinites" (THE WORLD FINISHED).

"The New Gods"—Energy.

Adventure-pictures: "Hunting an Error"—" *The Rise and Fall of the Word*"—"The Ubiquitous," destroys form (logic, beauty)—trust—credulity. Meaning of the search for discipline through abstract symbols—*Babel*, Pentecost. The magical (or harmonic) use, and the functional use, the "rational."

Anecdote

Export trade in gods.

There was a quarter of workshops in which gods were made for other people. There were sculptors in wood, stone, and marble; painters of ikons.

And, according to the faiths of their customers, they fashioned Baals, Hermeses, monsters, virgins, Venuses.

There were writers' stalls too, where they scrawled out holy books, hermetic texts, formularies of prayer.

Thus in this privileged isle was brought together in one place all that had subsisted apart and in mutual ignorance, divided in both time and space and scarcely to be conceived otherwise; an experiment which, in its previous attempt, at Babel, had wretchedly miscarried.

They tried out all these diverse products upon the same experimental subjects.

Morals.

*

There were menticurists who were to the mind, and language, what manicurists are to the hands, and, in the late mornings while the latter were busy about trimming and polishing the nails of those whose concern was for their bodies, the mind-setters would interrogate them and beguile them with subtlety of thought and elegance of discourse. They taught them how to pronounce, to employ the tones of the voice, to abstain from terms that were too vulgar or too abstract, and to form complete sentences; and they opened their eyes to ideas, concerning which they insisted that they should retain solely those they had made really their own, advising them to show all others the door and not to imagine they were thinking when they were merely repeating in other words what they had read or heard somewhere.

*

The Speaking Head with closed eyes gives forth oracles, etc.

A traveler embarks upon a dialogue with it.

And it speaks with total objectivity...in aphorisms. Without *I*, like a sort of calculation.

No one's voice.

Repeats always in its own manner whatever has just been

said to it, and then transforms it by successive regulated changes.

> It opens an eye!
> Its amazement.
> No questions allowed.

*

A man was certain of something. No one could think what to do with him. They put him in turn into prison, into a pulpit, onto the throne, into a lunatic asylum; they thought of killing him. Others wished to force him to fertilize a thousand chosen women. In the end, weary of all these metamorphoses, he announced that he was certain of nothing, and was left in peace. He took this opportunity to write an "Ethics," which is one of the most influential books in the world. For everybody speaks of it and quotes from it, but no one has read it.

*

The temples of the *true gods*:

Fear, Hunger, Desire, Diseases, Cold. . . .

The true gods are the powers and potentialities of the *senses*.

*

> Monuments. INSCRIPTIONS.
>   Style.
> Treatment of the Sun—colloquial
> Worship. The god visible but dazzling.
> "With us, god is essentially deniable."

Life was found in the island of Xiphos as copper is at Tharsis, incense and cinnamon at. . . .

Life of a fine and potent quality, the product of exceptionally favorable conditions.

Their instincts formidably keen; their sensibility extraordinary. Their intelligence both simple and disciplined—and all these combining or remaining distinct according to simple laws. . . .

In one of the squares of Xiphos was to be seen a flat surface of polished agate, watched over by one who was scholar rather than sage, and upon which rolled endlessly from face to face a strange polyhedron cut in such a manner that it could find no position of rest.

Elsewhere a strange egg danced as if alive at the crest of a jet of water.

The fountains were ingenious and set problems. Some sang.

Motto

That what is may be

This would be one of the inscriptions over one of the gates, literally but not well translated:

Go out to come in

(concern yourself not to know what you know, in order to know how you know it and to know your knowing)

*

An island without shame—where all go naked, and not merely naked but as free with the body everywhere as we are with our uncovered faces, our mouths, our hands.

*

9-2

A monument all of whose successive shadows, and all the shadows of whose parts, were beautiful, making changing designs. A sort of building casting a silhouette.

*

This solitary tried out upon himself all the poisons of abstract language. Upon others he tried out the word God.
　　Xiphos, isle of ? simplicians.

*

Medicine at Xiphos:
　　Longevity—with preservation.
　　Prolongation of life with prolongation of the values of life

　　The wise men. Marriage—after training.

　　The synthetic animals.

Justice:
　　Politics and Economics. People who could not agree were shut up together in the same prison until they could.
　　This worked wonders.

*

Isle found by chance, floating, repelled by every other body.

Energy:
　　They had a special sort of electricity.
　　Religion, mysteries.
　　Ways and Means.
　　"A shipwreck put us in possession of your sciences, our own are entirely different."

*

Fair at Xiphos:

    "The recipes of the Great Lambert"
            or the **M**
        infallible means

    of. . . .

Here insert things desirable but beyond the reach of techniques and sciences:

    To make oneself loved (a classic requirement)

    To make beautiful things

                etc.

A singular fair this was.

    Sideshows of monsters—and what monsters!

    The Hermaphrodite

    The spirital* Herculeses

A literary and philosophical fair; for . . . yes, indeed!

    We too are an exhibition of freaks.

Narrative: "I had scarcely left P's exhibition when suddenly, on the embankment, I was carried away in spirit and found myself amidst all the kaleidoscopic hurly-burly of a Fair. Fake savages, bogus monsters, soothsayers."

                *

Xiphos—isle of wonders.

    The artisans—and the intelligent or intellectuals.

    The former had very different notions about matter from ours, and the latter had equally different ones about mind.

    The artisans worked upon matter with their very souls, which knew how to find the way into their work and to live wholly in their hands; the intellectuals seemed through language and symbol to have the same control of their ideas as the athlete, acrobat, conjurer, juggler, do of their limbs.

* Fr. *espiritels.*—J.M.

(The scent-maker.) The smith hammered out rhythms and forms. The jeweler held his gems to the light and then seemed to extract them from his own eyes and to mount them. The painter danced his painting and the sculptor battled with clay or stone, a fight ever more furious and at closer quarters. Now he leapt backward, hand withdrawn; now he leapt forward, hand outstretched. The naked potter shaped his vase as a lover makes and remakes the body of his mistress; and the glass-blower sighed his desire into the molten bubble —*spirabat*.

The philosopher would suddenly overturn his own thought in discourse and without ceasing to follow it and bind it to itself. They were either rooted as trees or walking without the power to stop.

The geometer felt within himself all space, etc. . . . and dazzling transformations.

And the poet sang his words, becoming one with language —as the musician inhabited a world of sound.

The useful was taken for granted.

The useless was all that mattered.

Stones fell inadvertently as if hurled at random.

And the laws of nature seemed grotesque.

They explained that these laws were a fantasy acted out.

Acem

This is a tale that comes to me every time I pass through the quarter where is,

where live what have not been destroyed by venality, nor brutishness, nor the superstitions of hygiene, nor politics

nor by the architect, nor the engineer, nor the city councillor, nor the building contractor, nor the health inspector, nor anybody you like to think of

there is a balcony that all these fellows keep an eye on without knowing it

it is unaware of this.

with it an art dies

putting up a building in the year 1200 or 1600 demanded talent and the sense of form in almost all who were engaged upon it, apart from mere laborers who provided nothing but their strength of arm. The others were each concerned with some special material known intimately to hand and eye—stone, wood, lead—that they worked up from the raw.

The construction of a present-day building asks almost nothing in the way of individual intelligence. Invention, taste, conception are one man's alone, and in general he does not trust in his imagination, if he has one, and isn't afraid of it.

*

There was a man named Assem, Azem, or Acem. He was fat and white, very handsome, his features were harmoniously matching curves—his nose was strongly reminiscent of a scimitar and his eyebrows, thin and black as wire, were two arcs drawn with a brush. His eyes were profoundly clear, the pupils mere pinpoints of black—except that at times these dilated extraordinarily, and then the black devoured all. He had very beautiful hands, they were white and soft; the one, overwhelmed rather than merely loaded with rings, familiarly caressed the other (which was quite bare) as though it belonged to someone else.

He never laughed; he never walked: or at any rate no one had ever seen him other than firmly ensconced in a small upholstered armchair, into which he appeared to have been built. As I say, he never laughed; when he ought to have laughed, he clapped his lids shut and tossed back his head. He spoke slowly, with an extreme economy both of words and of intonation; he articulated each syllable, giving it some musical value that was very sensitive and remarkable. What he said was brief, consisting always of a simple question and answer. He gave no impression of reasoning, he cared nothing for being consistent. Most probably he considered what we call logic, rational sequence in ideas, as fit for nothing except the practical—and even there frequently disastrous. Indeed Assem for the most part limited himself, instead of speaking, to a series of musical notes conformable to what he was thinking or feeling. Their timbre was always grave and ironic. Yet, in spite of this semi-mutism, conversation with him was always a good deal more than interesting. It was regularly of the highest importance, for one derived from the company of this distinctly peculiar person a certain inestimable benefit. This was that one could lay out before him an idea, a thesis, a plan for a book or a business, the scheme of a journey or some other enterprise, even a proposed law; and thanks to his mere silence (which was however a silence with illustrations, the dilatation of his pupils, the lowering of his lids, the rhythm of the bedizened hand gliding caressingly over the hand that was naked, one or all of these) it was seldom indeed that by a sort of divination one had not soon laid bare the flaw, petty folly, self-contradiction, lapse in taste or fault in timing or incoherence or uselessness or plain banality in whatever one had laid before him. Without opening his mouth, he had said everything. He raised objections, so to speak, at a distance, within the very intelligence that was submitting to him its creation. He pinpointed the absurd by a mere act of presence.

Almost nothing was known of his origins, family, and means of subsistence, not even whether he lived alone or with others. As for his habits, it goes without saying that every kind of assorted malicious rumor was bandied about among the few who were admitted into his circle. A species of celebrity hovered over him, extending far among the cultured inhabitants of the town. He was reckoned to have been a doctor; but was equally held to display the indelible tokens of the spoiled priest. One day he was compared, most felicitously, to Maelzel's famous mechanical chess player. Someone then made a sufficiently coarse allusion (but delicately expressed) as to what could have been the love life of that automaton—a jibe obviously pointed at Assem. For my part, I shrugged my shoulders: I know too well that truth and reality never boast more than the slenderest connection. Truth is a turn of phrase: it has doubt for a beginning, and for an end verification. But reality is simply what it is, in other words precisely what denies or conceals itself from phrasing: no one can say where it begins or ends, and to claim to represent it is as idle an attempt as that of the painter, who depicts faces or objects by means of strokes unknown to nature, where are neither lines nor planes.... All the same, I confess that Assem's hidden life gave me food for thought. Never have I found in one man so many enigmas. The real quality of his intellect, his deepest likings, his inner nature, his finances, his past—all these were so many tormenting conundrums. I will even add that I was at times dubious of his very sex.... In a word, after several months of almost daily attendance upon him, I had reached a state in which the sole desire and hope of my life was simply to get him to explain himself once and for all. I dreamt only of how to extract from this demi-mute the avowals that would release me from this obsession.

Sometimes it would happen, in the middle of a conversation to which he was contributing only the signals and vestigial remarks of which I have spoken, that he would fall asleep or seem to fall asleep, an act that produced in those about him not merely surprise but uneasiness. What gave him the appearance of being awake was the extraordinary look in his eyes, which gazed fixedly and wide-open not, so it seemed, upon things and persons actually in the room but upon all such as conceivably might have been. At these times his pupils grew so huge that the too clear irises foundered in twin pools of utter black.

And then what happened, happened. At the very extremity of a long day, when no more could be distinguished in the room than the contrast between light and dark, and I had fallen into a deeply protracted silence, worn out by hour upon hour in which I had displayed before Assem endless ideas for whose sake I wished to avail myself of the curious properties of his presence that I have already detailed, and that enabled me to form my own opinion within myself upon them, Assem suddenly enunciated, almost under his breath, the two syllables MARA. At once an unknown voice spoke in the next room, saying AMOR, in the mode of a question, to which Assem replied AMOR. The curtain of the left doorway was lifted aside, the door opened, but nothing came through it. I heard the door on the right hand open, I gazed, but nothing came through it. Then I looked at Assem, who uncrossed his hands and, his face perfectly expressionless, indicated with an equal and symmetrical gesture of each of them the one door and the other. This aroused an indefinable sense of impending mystery in me and, while he resumed his statuesque pose once more, various distinct interpretations of these occurrences came to my mind. Gradually, as if upon a sort of musical stave drawn parallel to this game of speculation, and as if in another time than that one, a kind of sketch of a general theory that might cover the diverse possible explanations of this little scene whose elements were one person and two opening doors began to take shape within me.

This *me* took up the interior attitude that we may represent by "What does it mean?": and at this sign—or perhaps rather *under* this sign—I was invaded by a somewhat disorderly concourse of those creatures commonly called ideas.

"An open door and an open door, Assem between them: is not this surely an allegory of the possible? Or rather a kind of an invitation to something or other that should come? After all, what are these doors to me?" I thought of the past and the future that they could signify.

At this juncture Assem repeated the gesture that he had just made, then, crossing his arms, with his right hand he indicated the door at the left, and with his left hand the door at the right. Then he replaced them in their original position. And now from the left door there entered a young man, and from the right door a young woman, each of whom seemed to me possessed of a remarkable beauty. Both greeted me graciously, then went to Assem, and each embraced one of his knees. Upon this I saw him open his arms and clasp them both to him.

Startled and deeply disturbed by this strange and wholly unexpected tableau of intimacy, which smacked of ritual, something from a private and perhaps ambiguous liturgy, my first instinct was to leave at once. But I dared not. I was paralyzed by the fear of seeming to retreat, and there was also in this irresolution a distinct and culpable craving to see what could happen next. Anyway, I took the course of least resistance: I closed my eyes.

After a time I could hear a voice, the rare voice of Assem—that voice which he appeared to hoard as though he reckoned that we have only a certain finite number of words to speak during our lives, and he had discovered this number, and had found out that the length of a life depends on it (whereas we on the contrary fancy that the number depends on the length of life) and is like a fortune to which one can add nothing and which lasts only as long, or as little, as the miserliness or extravagance of its possessor determines.

... Now this voice was that of a little child. And it was saying, "Love me; you, love me, and you too, love me!" and then it added in a whisper, "That's the most idle and useless word in the world."

And next I heard a groan that made me shudder, the triple groan of the group that I did not want to see. And then a long silence was broken by the voice of the young man, a strong clear voice but dark and as if held in: "How can you wish that we should love you? We feel the purest hate for you, we hate you with all our being. We are said to be beautiful and no doubt we are, by the reckoning of what passes for beauty among mortals. But don't we know, precisely because we are so, that we could and that we should be a hundred, a thousand times more beautiful than we are? What have you done with the precious seed of your creative will? Why did you not cast into the female scale of our destiny the full weight of the energies of perfection?"

He was silent. And the voice of the young woman was raised in its turn, a voice more sharply sweet than the finest and sweetest needle: "Assem, Assem, and why did you so arrange it that we could not love one another, he and I? We are brother and sister, yet all that we are asks that we should share a common bed and that nothing more should separate us than those differences that feed the godlike struggles toward union. But you see that we are rivals and that I hate my brother bitterly, for he wants all that I want, he possesses what I possess, and we have nothing to envy each other for, we who could love one another so tenderly."

*

I felt the strongest impulse to get up and go; and yet at the same time this was strangely impossible, and I stayed. I felt that I had been reduced to a dead dumb thing, involuntary witness of an incomprehensible scene.

*

"You are my fault," said Assem, "and as a fault I love you, and as a fault I hate you. Between us three there is a pact of flesh and spirit."

*

Suddenly I perceived that this so pitiable group had fused into a single mass, a scarcely begun sculpture of which the play of the dying light could still just suggest the modeling. . . . Day declined. . . . I realized, or I fancied, that each of the three persons who constituted this mass had closed his eyes—a natural enough idea and yet it struck me as strange, upon reflection. I, I felt myself insidiously constrained to veil my own. The passing of the light aroused in me an indefinable desire to follow suit or match it, involuntarily, with an attenuation of my own faculty of sight, opposing to things a force of intellect that would counterbalance and end them.

Soon we were FOUR, unquestionably, there in the total dark. . . .

It was an unbearable condition. An intimacy with life itself. . . . Here were, I felt, four "inner lives."

THE SCREEN

A story. The tale of someone who would be shown (at determined junctures of the narrative) seated in his armchair, smoking, his gaze involuntarily glued to a screen, a door, or wall—or upon some smallish object. Then ideas about things, about recent introductions into his life (matter of the *narrative*), anxieties, adumbrations, intimate themes, the beginnings of discoveries, etc., would display themselves *on* or *as if on* this screen—where they would be both *within him* and *before him*, under mutual observation, protagonists of a complex monologue.

The recurrence of this motif in a narrative would act as its formal and ornamental law—a very true one, for that matter. The moment—the phase of tête-à-tête with the screen or small familiar object, the half-dream of the *present-real*, the *proximate-real*, and the *possibilities*—would constitute itself, *on the other hand*, a sufficiently stable element of form.

The view of the screen, and the views beside it.

The past and future, at the expense of the present.

Times of emotion—regrets, sighs, tendernesses, purities, exaggerations. Perhaps one could "construct" a pattern of these moments, a general formula.

And, at the conclusion of these fragments, a resolution, more or less definitive. Certain themes reinforced—implanted —happy discoveries—formulas adopted—rubbings-out.

And then return to the present. The wall reappears. The focus of consciousness moves back *onto the object*.

*

Seen by an angel, the pattern of our habits (with all the private rituals and sealed orders, the bizarre associations and psychosomatic signaling, that underlie them) would have the appearance of some strange ceremonial of restrictions and imposed conditions—though perceptible only when it is disturbed.

This system extends and multiplies upon itself whenever life takes on some periodicity—as a crystal forms in a liquid that is at rest and amenable to the *natural* order of things.

Truly, he who should study at close quarters a single day in the life of a man, without letting himself be deceived by the psychic broadcasting and loud-mouthed self-importance of the inner life and of the comedy in which it takes part, would enjoy a spectacle: the substitution of the most universal for the most particular, of the mechanical for seeming fantasy.

*

Acem said: I am forever what at the moment I am. [Another door opens.]* This my *moment* I call my *forever*. And you? How can you do or say otherwise? Would it not be lying or trying to persuade that one is other than one is, other than one's *every moment*? Is one not *forever* between two open doors, going out through the one, and through the other entering in?

RITUAL

To each his own "sacrament."

In each man's sphere, points of negative field—Death, amongst the civilized, is as it were *outside nature*—and this brings on false ideas of life, upsetting our notions of the values of natural signs. Cf. certain excesses of "moral" sensibility. Points of high sensitivity—perhaps as quasi-accidental as the especially tender spots of the body, that can pain us out of all proportion to their organic importance.

The spontaneously ritualistic in people's lives, which takes its place of its own accord—in the half-tenebrous regions of their existence.

*

* In the margin of the MS.—J.M.

I know (he said), by a method of calculation previously quite unknown—I know, to within a few dozens, the number of words that I shall have spoken between my first babblings and my dying discourse.

Every word I speak therefore, I grudge it, as an irrecoverable expense.

In no way can one evade the fact that this number is finite, say N. If *n* is the number of words already *lost*, then N minus *n* remain to me.

*

The twin children:
O my evolutions....
The two serpents.
The one Dominatio—The other Virtus.

I have begotten you to know myself better, and that I may give you to each other.

For no matter how discerning a man may be, how deeply receptive to the sensation of himself and to the knowledge of his own thought, nevertheless his acuteness cannot penetrate that part of his substance that is *datum*; and there is *much more in us than us—much more is needed to make me than I. Personality* is no more than one of the side effects of one's being. The I is a continuous by-product of a flux of quite a different nature.

*

Metaphysics.

(*Spinoza*)

He has his chessboard.
God, the universe, matter, spirit, chessmen.
  The doppelgänger playing against himself.
                Faculty of not being *one*.
                Importance of unknowing oneself
                in order to conceive and to play
                against the *I*.

*

The ox on the (virtual) tongue.
  forbids thought.
But the will necessary to impose *inner silence*, because it immobilizes those potentialities necessary to inner language, implies a thought running counter to the intention which must be realized by stages.
  Silence within.

Poem

O WE...
O YOU, O I,
The Past and Future are our foremost foes.
Loving is poison, thinking
Comes always to a bad end:
(Impotence gets it, or terror).
We need all ignorance to live.

So spoke. And so kept silence
He of whose presence I was well possessed.
And slowly the adamant mirror of
My troubled fascination cleared.
An idea of suavity or of
The depth of a deep rose respired
Suddenly in my thought, conveying
Fresh warmth of life.

And my heart told me: Close your eyes,
Forget the Beasts and Angels! Does
Your frame not tremble, and your flesh
Not cease to be the same?
And my heart told me: Open your arms,
And let your hands in the stretch of space
Guess and finger and caress,
Clutch and handle, pluck and seize,
As if a lyre, as if an urn.

Fragments

... I would make a model town—or rather a town that specialized in calm and in meticulously perfect personal work, whether manual or not.

Rigorously proscribed in this town would be all noisy machines, news, publicity, the cinema, radios, private telephones—and politics.

As a general rule, all that rudely speeds life up and interrupts the flow of ideas or of occupations, investing every life with the tempo of a troubled mind.

Moreover a firm control would be exercised over everything offered for sale. Its quality would be checked on; and sometimes its nature. All factory-produced foodstuffs would be forbidden.

Cocktails, canned goods.

TOWN OF CALM

In those days I had the good fortune to visit an extraordinary town, founded in Manitoba by one Dick Bouchedor with permission of the federal authority.

One could only get into it by staircases or by lifts. On

entry one had to sign a declaration of total submission to the rules; one deposited one's jewels and money and was given receipts and a check book.

No pianos, no radios, no gramophones, no pets.

No newspaper ever penetrated.

All publicity absolutely forbidden.

No telephone.

No wires.

*

... In this language (of Betelgeuse) certain words were so difficult to articulate and to accent that most people did not attempt them and it more or less took a virtuoso, of great natural gifts, to. . . .

These words were the most important. Amongst them, presumably, the names of the Gods—and of the elements of the Universe.

This virtual veto had notable consequences that deeply affected public affairs and. . . .

*

In those days

The Sages were gathered together without knowing it: no matter where they might be living in the world, *the same thought* struck them, borne in upon each by different considerations, based by each upon different premises, and guided to the same conclusion by means, images, fashions, incidents, memories, routes, and occasions that differed entirely.

United, ignorant of it, they all thought together, like a single intelligence at the climax of a long self-deliberation.

*

The Emperor's architects, commanded to build him a palace a thousand cubits *square*, began to lay out the site. They measured a base-line AB: but on remeasuring it for safety, found it a different length; and this happened a number of times. Moreover, when they tried to measure it in the opposite direction, they found that $BA = AB$. All the values of AB fell between p and p', and those of BA between q and q'. So they decided to take an average. But then each side yielded a different average; and furthermore they found their would-be right angles equally deceiving. For the magician had said, "Never will you build your palace." *He had merely ensured by a spell that the variability of matter should become perceptible.*

VARIETY

It rained, and sparse drops fell like notes from fingers reaching for a melody. At times, a sudden inspiration, a gust whipped a fine spray across my eyes and stung them. Wandering on foot and in mind, I let my paces lose me, straying deeper and deeper into old streets that grew more roundabout, ever less and less capable of leading me where once perhaps I had had the intention to go. Roads sometimes do with us what they will. I had forgotten the very principle of my route and had begun to feel uncertain even of the hour, the day. My goal was mislaid; and with it, my sense of time; and with my sense of time, everything of my epoch and of myself—all that had been, all that would be, my age and the world, dissolving into this wet tail-end of morning as I drifted between the old mansions that had seen better days. I do not altogether know what is meant by "revery," and I do not care for this word for it always makes me think of spineless writing; it fills me with the ennui, indeed with the disgust, that I feel for poetry prostituted to the taste of silly minds. My glance, or my thought, in either case my *very instant*, skipped, halted, flew on, from some carved stone or from one of those wrought-iron balconies in which I find such art, to some inkling of an idea, the germ of an essay or of a poem, a word accompanied by some snatch of etymology, the prick of some vexation, the first or the last visitation of one of those objects of the intellect or of the heart that constitute the bric-à-brac, the junk shop, of a human existence. These gleams of the mind that flared and were extinguished, these strange vacua, unmotivated stoppings, aimless starts; between them they composed a being of pure caprice whose life I was living, breathing the douches of freshness that the small rain, worried by the wind. . . .

A JOURNEY TO THE LAND OF FORM

I have just returned from a country far removed from our own, in several senses. They have a singular system of law and order, precise and   regulations, a spirit . . .

I trembled with fear and admiration. . . . Hardly had I descended from the vehicle that took me there than I was struck with the extreme good manners of its citizens and the forthrightness of their dealings. Everyone was smiling. Drivers, porters, shopkeepers, intermediaries of every kind, eagerly attentive. I was soon obliged to instruct myself in their manners; as a stranger I was granted some breathing-space, but was not allowed to fall behind in my progress.

I learned then that in this extraordinary country errors in language are jumped upon very smartly. The penalties are dire—one solecism too many can land one in solitary confinement. Posters and all public notices are strictly inspected. (Authors are. . . .)

Offenses against logic, sophistries, irresponsible or violent statements, these all lead to the police court. Even I, a foreigner, was severely admonished for jumping to a conclusion.

In short, all that is meant to work by violent, or seductive, or illusive means upon our minds or senses is treated in that land as any violent action upon the body is treated in others. They hold that the eyes, ears, imaginations, memories, and reasoning faculties of their citizens ought to be just as much respected as their goods, indeed as though they were their most precious possessions.

Odds and Ends

London Bridge

A LITTLE WHILE ago I was walking across London Bridge and I paused to contemplate what is for me an endless pleasure—the sight of a rich, thick, complex waterway whose nacreous sheets and oily patches are loaded with a confusion of ships, their white smoke-puffs, their swinging davits, their strange balancing-acts with crates and bales, bringing themselves and the whole panorama to life.

My eyes halted me; I leaned upon my elbows, as if in the grip of a vice. Delight of vision held me with a ravenous thirst, involved in the play of a light of inexhaustible richness. But endlessly pacing and flowing at my back I was aware of another river, a river of the blind eternally in pursuit of immediate material object.

This seemed to me no crowd of individual beings, each with his history, his private god, his treasures and his scars, his interior monologue and fate; rather I made of it, unconsciously, in the depths of my body, in the shaded places of my eyes, *a flux of identical particles*, equally sucked in by the same nameless void, their deaf headlong current pattering monotonously over the bridge. Never have I so felt solitude, in a mingling of pride and anguish—a strange and obscure sense of the danger of dreaming between the water and the crowd.

I found myself guilty of the crime of poetry upon London Bridge.

*

This *sidelong* unease expressed itself in a veiled threat. I could recognize the bitter flavor of an undefined guilt, as though I had committed some grave infringement of a hidden law, without the slightest memory of my offense or even of the rule in question. Was not I suddenly divorced from the living *if I for my part denied them their life?*

(These last words began to hum in my mind to an imaginary operatic air.)

There is something guilty in everyone who sets a distance. A man who thinks, thinks always *against* the habitable world. He takes away its function; he pushes his neighbor into the void.

This smoky port, this dirty splendid water, these pale gold skies, soiled, rich, and sad, exercised upon me such a force and virtue of fascination that, lost in the pleasure-house of sight while brushed against by a multitude of persons *with an aim*, I truly became something wholly different from them.

*

How does it come about that a spectator is suddenly ravished quite out of himself, so deeply altered that he falls abruptly into a world where all is *signification*, out of a world where all is simply *sign*? Things swiftly lose for him their ordinary properties, the points of recognition disappear. There are no more mental shortcuts, objects have lost their names practically; whereas in the normal state the world about us can be perfectly well replaced, in a *utilitarian* sort of way, by a world of symbols and labels. Do you see this world of arrows and letters? . . . *In eo vivimus et movemur.*

Sometimes, in an inexplicable rapture, our sensing over-powers our knowing. Intellect evaporates like a dream, and we find ourselves in an unknown country at the very nipple of the real and pure. And, as in an unknown country whose tongue is strange we hear only rhythms, tones, sonorities, stresses, ear-surprises, so do objects lose upon the instant all human and functional values and the spirit inhabits the country of the eyes alone. Thus, for a time which has limit but no measure (for what has been, what will be, what should be, are but empty signs), *I am that I am, I am that I see*, there and not there upon London Bridge.

Sketch

THE BRAIN left to its own devices is a craftsman of the Far East.

Dragons, fabulous beasts; infinite rigorous developments from arbitrary premises; and what open-work spheres held one within the other, and detached from one another, carved from the matter of memory!

As the Chinese with his lump of jade or ivory, so does the carver *Life* pursue his capricious ways into the block of the past, finding unending passages and illimitable surprises in that morsel of done time.

Dreams

Dream.

At waking my mind flies straightway from the near, to embark upon constructions in the world where building costs nothing, or next to nothing. Great activity is manifest in the demi-universe of imaginary fabrications and combinations. My desires create, they struggle to frame me what will exactly please. I upset their projects. I start again; I revise, I perfect.

A loud crash tumbles me from up there. I am cut in two. I find that I have fallen to precisely where my body lies. I perceive in myself two incompatible persons. Back and forth between these two presences there follows a regular oscillation of unknown period. I have interests in two worlds that have no communication between them. I dream *or* I wake. I see *or* I make. I take leave of my hands and my table for the structures and workshops of my excitement; I return to the real....

Little by little this double life begins to compose. The swinging of the pendulum *I* slows down. I consent to *be* and to *build*, more or less together. Some change has occurred. I pass from the state of alternate disturbance, the state of "the one or the other," to the state of "the one and the other." I have created an attention that can deal with two *postulated* worlds together.

If we could actually achieve a state comprising both waking and true dreaming, that would be a field for some fine discoveries. . . .

*

Dream.

Thirty years ago I dreamed this dream:

I was on a quay, at Rouen, toward sunset. A flaming, delicate rosy light upon the river, upon the cobbles, upon the edges, gangways, bulges, and projections of the ships at anchor.

But one thing only concerned me.

Ten yards away was a little pile of coal. A power emanated from it, an indefinable *virtue* that I felt strangely *weigh* upon me.

I felt myself hypnotized, paralyzed, constrained to its contemplation, as if completely *reoriented* within by this gloomy and glistening mass. This black cone, of sable diamond, was for me like the Magnetic Mountain of the Arabian Nights.

And something in me *put a name* to this singular effect, without hesitation. Something in me knew, with a certain and immediate knowledge, that this was the *Gaze of Napoleon*.

IMUS

Dream opera.

A great lamp, the color of pearl and dream, emits a glow or a music, gentle and soft. The growing light, *or* the harmony that swells into complexity, illumines *or* creates the scene little by little. *One* detects *Imus* seated before a table. *One* sees him *or One* is him. The better *one* distinguishes him, the more *one* is him. The harmony forms *or* evokes, from *one* knows not what distance, a young blonde servant girl, full of grace. She approaches Imus, leans on her elbows, then half sits beside him, *on nothing*, quite close and clear. *One* knows her face, yet does not see it, for it stays turned away, *an abstract thing*; and the smile *one* knows she has hangs through all the shadowy room, like a perfume. But her warm body, the life of nape and elbow, presses, imposing itself.

This contact is inexpressibly real. The whole world *perceives through Imus* who is also the whole world; and *one* understands, in contradiction, that the vision of this young girl is no more than a figuring or accessory illusion.

She says nothing for longer than one can reckon, infinitely gentle beside Imus; but the astonishment of her arrival, of this pose, of this approach and this silence, takes possession of him, takes possession of the scene, the room, or me, just as they had been possessed by the smile *or* the perfume.

No word, no movement either of the girl or of another, dissipate or disturb the unease growing within Imus and, by the mysterious *agency of the presence of Imus*, within all the world *or* in me. This contact casts a spell on flesh and heart, on the real hidden human presence, making the glow and the musical whisper dimmer, softer, spreading a dark and cloying gleam, altering plans and duties, clouding all natural prudence, lighting one inclination alone. An ever-thickening curtain rolls across the rest of the world with a continuous rumble, utterly pleasurable and utterly troubling at once.

Dream. Shipmaster's Report.

One is at sea, lying in a bunk; two bodies in one; narrowly joined, and *one* wonders whether one or two, because of this constriction of the exiguous bed of the cabin. This onefold and twofold creature is prey to an infinite sadness, a pain and tenderness that is *with him*, without limits or cause. A storm wind howls in the night outside. The ship rolls and groans terribly. Creature latches to creature and *one* is aware of the anguished beating of a single heart, the dull thuds of the engine thumping and struggling with the sea, the regular poundings, ever more violent, of the raging waves upon the hull.

Terror, danger, tenderness, anguish, the yawing, the force of the waves, grow to a *breaking point*.

And at last the catastrophe is come. The hatches give way, the very wall parts, spewing deadly water.

I wake. *My face is bathed in tears.* They have rolled down my cheeks, to my lips, and my first sensation is the taste of their salt, which doubtless has just evoked this whole desperate complex of tenderness, sorrow, and sea.

*

Note.

One will have noticed that several times in this sort of "Shipmaster's Report" I have underlined the word *One*. I have often noticed the importance of this pronoun, indeed the necessity of using it, in the accounts that we give of dreams. Such accounts are always suspect. We know our dreams only in the translation that waking makes of them—in a state that is totally incompatible with them. I think that we are totally incapable of conveying to ourselves the essential *unmeaning* and constitutional incoherence of dreams. But the text of our naïve translations not infrequently betrays between its lines the hesitations and puzzlements of the translator, his periphrases out of the world of waking. Such disturbances among the forms of meaning make me think of those slight irregularities and anomalies from whose analysis astronomers infer the existence of invisible bodies....

The word *One*, that I have had to employ, stands for an indistinct *subject*, at once spectator, author, audience, actor, in whom the seeing and the seen, the active and the passive, are reunited and even strangely compounded. They are repugnant to our language, these psychic possibilities so far removed from our habits *of useful thought*. It cannot express them. But perhaps in some dialect of an Australian or Red Indian tribe one might discover terms and forms more varied, more complex, more general, in a word more *learned* than our own, by which to translate more satisfactorily closely the shapeless and nonhuman phenomena of dream.

*

Athalie.

Madame T. lost her niece a few months ago.

She dreamed that she was in her drawing room taking tea with a friend, and suddenly the dead niece came in.

Surprised and overjoyed, she rose to welcome her. The woman who was with her looked, stood up, and *vanished*. The dead woman embraced her aunt. Then she seized her round the waist and made as if to fly off with her into the air.

But the dreamer, the *I* of this dream, found herself clasped only by a body that crumpled, turned to water, dissolved. Soon there was no more than at her feet an unspeakable rag, a dead garment—all that was needed to awake her in an excess of horror.

*

11-2

Note.

In certain moods one fancies verses to be extraordinarily beautiful which, a few hours or even a few seconds later, one recognizes as atrocious. One has been dreaming.

If, as a thoroughly up-to-date myth would have it, the poet is really a dreamer, one wagers that he can never reread himself without groaning.

I remember having been thoroughly distressed, for the course of a whole morning, at being unable to salvage some verses heard in a dream, which had left me with the impression of an incomparable beauty, as if infinite, singular, impersonal. I am expressing this as well as I may.

But I taught myself consolation, gently and little by little, by a sort of analysis ever finer and more searching, in that these beautiful lines might not, indeed could not, have been anything other than a meaningless stammering, mere syllabification, *plus* a sensation of unheard-of marvels. . . . A pure, or an accidental, coincidence between a random local babbling and the unmotivated feeling of a state of enchantment.

*

Suicide may be compared to the desperate gesture made by a dreamer to break his nightmare. He who by an effort escapes from an evil sleep, *kills*; he kills his dream, *he kills himself as dreamer.*

Lost Verses

Heart of night.

Intermittent night, almost too beautiful, of blacks too black and lights too biting; marvel of possession and of vanishment, night of admirable asides; *no moment that is not all or nothingness.*

On the breast of night, in the night's center.
The mind's wakefulness well poised against the
  substance of the night:
Notably alone, distinct, at rest.
Apart from the night, sharply dividing her powers!
Then the darkness lightens it,
Silence speaking near:
Then the weightless body in the calm
Knows itself to the last promontories of foot and
  finger:
And all language is there,
And all remembrance is there,
And all the mind's movements and operations
Are there to be felt and seen:
And the idols are ranged
By genus, order, class, and category,
And knowledge is known, not *things....*

*

The heard.

Listen to this delicate endless susurration which is silence.
Hear what is heard when nothing is heard.

*

All is gone under the sand of silence.

The story of all my delights and desires is a dead city,
erased and enlaced in desert cinder.

But hear this lone far pure whistling, creating space, as if
alone it existed, of itself, to its depth.

*

Now nothing. But this nothing is huge in the ears.

Still whistling. Sinister whistling; regular, endless, un-
changing monotone whistling; unwinding thread of time
losing itself in the universe of the heard, consubstantial with
space, running toward eternal expectation, filling the swelling
sphere with the desire to hear it.

*

The birds.

First birds. At last their little cries are born. Life and
plurality of life in the highest heaven.

Little cries of birds little scissor-snips, the small clicks of
scissors in the peace. But what a seam of silence to be unsewn!

*

Reversible action.

Indeed a sort of happiness basks within fatigue. Fatigue of
repose, infinite extension, the limits of the body and the
limits of the world compounded.

I dissolve into the soft warmth of my bed. To the man who turns and tosses between sleep and waking all things are possible. He can stretch to right or left. The substance of his luck is still molten; his dreams come bidden to hand. Beyond the barrier he sees his powers and his acts.

*

Renewal.

Trundlings of first wheels. Trudging off to their labors, the early ghosts cough and gossip in the presumable street. On the dung, there must be fresh sun.

O life, O painting upon darkness!
Radiant morning, you are painted upon the night.
Delicious morning, you paint yourself upon the night.
These swallows flit like sounds dying.
So high the bird flies that the eyes turn upward to the
very springs of tears.

MORNING

Waking.

How gentle the light at waking, how lovely this living blue!
The word "Pure" opens my lips.
That is the name I give you.
Here, linked to the day that never yet has been, are the perfect thoughts that never will be. Seeds, eternal seeds, the highest general plane of existence and action.
The Universal is a seed, the Universal experienced without particulars, the Universal awaking sketchily in the gold, unblemished yet by individual affect.

I am born everywhere, far from this Identity, in every sparkling of light upon this hem, this fold, the edge of this thread, that mass of lucent water. As yet and effortlessly you are no more than a delicious effect of light and expectation, a miracle of fire silk smoke and slate, a complication of simple noises, a gilding and a murmuration, O day!

*

Why should I not delay my being I, and idle in the universal?

Why this morning should I choose myself? Why must I shoulder again my goods and ills? Suppose I were to abandon my name, my faiths, my habits, and my chains, like the dreams of my night, as one who, wishing to disappear and begin again, leaves carefully at the water's edge his clothes and papers?

Is not this the present lesson of my dreams, the prompting of my waking? And this morning, this summer morning, is it not the moment of imperious counsel to be like myself no more? Sleep has shuffled the deck; my dreams have muddled all, all's in suspension. . . .

At waking there is a period of birth, a bringing to birth of all things before one thing can take place. One is very naked before one dresses again.

*

The soul gulps down a mouthful of liberty from the spring, a mouthful of *uncommitted beginnings*.

It is a Certitude, this blue. This Sun whose very appearance signals a general turnout and salutes from all hands, who makes the leaf sing and the bridge shine, and all the brass bands of the sea; he is announced, and climbs into his judge's chair. He summons the pale illusions to his court, he condemns dreams, transports the fancies of the night, quashes the judgments of terror: he is the fear and hope of every mental thing.... What thoughts run underground, what procedures of the mind are at once struck to naught!

THE TREE

The tree sings like a bird.

Suddenly a gust—rough wind.

It blows, drops, comes again in waves.

On the great tree the wind confers a host of thoughts, surprises, troubles it, disturbs, attacks it everywhere. It clothes it in the million undersides of its own leaves. It weds it, altering it into a noise that swells, then slackens and becomes a dying stream.

It confers upon it the pure dream of the stream.

The tree dreams that it is stream.

It dreams itself a living spring in air....

Little by little the wind changes the tree into a poem, a pure line of verse....

*

I analyze and blend with the shivering of the little leaves of the huge tree that lives in my window. It begins and stops. The tree grown calm, I seek and find one small leaf quivering still.

Renewal now, speeded renewal. Hemidemisemiquavers, unsustainable trills. We are at the limits of the shrill. It is a spasm, a nervous tic, a St. Vitus dance, a delirium of over-excitation that seizes the central masses and menaces the whole huge life.

There is a manifest harmony between the crazy shaking of the leaf, and those of the stalk, the twig, the mother branch, the mighty ancestral bough. The heaviest slowly, gently, rocks itself; and the others, the finer they are the more they dance and throb and twinkle.

The movement gathers force from top to bottom.

An exquisite diminuendo resolves the crisis and the poetry lesson.

SINGING BIRDS

The bird cries or sings; and its voice means something quite different to the bird from what the growls or barkings of other beasts mean to them.

Only man and birds sing.

I mean not merely melody but what melody has in it of free activity, beyond the moment's needs.

The cry of an animal is meaning; he discharges some excess of pain or power, and no more.

The braying of the ass, the bellowing of the bull, the baying of the dog, the belling or troating of the stag, tell no more than their state, their hunger, their rut, their wound, or their impatience. These voices arise from the practical; we understand them with ease, for we possess their like.

But just as it soars and tumbles in space, choosing *in three dimensions* its routes at will, tracing at will between two given points an infinity of winged curves; and just as it foresees from on high and flies upon impulsion: so the Bird in its voice also is freer in its surroundings.

Song and mobility, a little less narrowly arranged for it by circumstance than for most other creatures.

MORNING

Morning. Rain of a disheveled dawn.

I gaze at the swift rain; I see it with all my skin.

The wind's caprice shifts clouds, and two or three minutes suffice wholly to change the face of the ocean's field. Suncolor and night-color mingle, or shift and replace each other. One stretch of the coast is dark and clear; another indecisively crumbled and melted into the wet material of vision. Vague soft rosy shapes.

These rapid transitions suggest those of an oversusceptible mind, still smiling over an idea though already more than half dominated by a sudden sadness or a sense of grim determination.

All that I see pictures to me the waverings of the spirit as it is invaded, then deserted, by the light and shade of ideas.

The swiftness of these transmutations of the seen is of the same numerical order as in those of the spirit. A "development" in music could express them with perfect exactness.

RENEWAL

I

Against the smoky gold of the horizon the sea is little by little defined; and from the rosy mountains, the soft and empty skies, from the confusion of foliage, walls, tiled roofs, and trails of smoke, from all this world in fact that now once more grows warm, renewing at a glance the bay, the fields, the magical fires of dawn, regretfully my eyes withdraw and become again the slaves of my table. It is another world, it is wholly another world, this world of the signs on my table. But to work! What an odd fencing-out of vision, what a parenthesis in space, what an enclave in the universe, is this page of mine all riddled with letters and muddled with scorings-out and overwritings! I read my lines between my lines and the asymptote of infinitely small successive approximations is as it were sketched upon the paper. Here the spirit chains itself to itself. Talents, errors, second thoughts, relapses —is it not here upon this scrap destined for the flames that the whole moral man appears? Through all the phases of self-trial, self-intoxication, self-release, self-loathing, self-mutilation, self-renewal, self-preservation, and self-love.

11

Intelligence. Pure watchfulness, Eternal impending, threat to all I desire! Blade that can flash from a cloud, how keenly I am aware of *imminence*! An unknown notion lurks already in the furrows of my brow. But I still remain apart from every notion, equally withdrawn from all the words and from all the constructions that are in me. My arrested eye gives no life to the object it sees; my ear hears nothing of what it hears. O my faceless presence, what a gaze is your gaze with neither object nor subject, what a power is your indefinable power that is the power in the air before a storm! I do not know what is preparing. I am love, and I am thirst, and have no name. For there is no man in man, and no I in I. But there will be an act without an actor, an effect without a cause, an accident which is my substance. The event that has no form nor time challenges every form and every time. It makes visible the invisible, it makes invisible what is seen. What it attracts, it devours; and what it destroys, it illumines....Here I am, I am prepared. Strike! Here I am, my inward eye fixed upon the blind spot of my expectancy.... From there the necessary event at times breaks forth and creates me.

Seas

INSCRIPTION ON THE SEA

MOST ANCIENT ELEMENT OF THE GLOBE, ALONE
  INTACT,
EVERYTHING SHE TOUCHES IS RUIN,
EVERYTHING SHE LEAVES IS NEW:
SHE WHO WITHDRAWS HERSELF BETWEEN TWO
  GIVINGS
BITTERLY GIVES AND WITHDRAWS.

*

Waves.

The wind stripes the big wave with little waves across it. The skin of the great ground-swell wrinkles in the superficialities of the breeze; and the mighty form rolling from far origins loses simplicity, grows complex, faceted, a crystal figure in endless transformation emitting the sound of boiling with its many inward cries, its rippings and bruisings, the plaitings and blendings of its waterstrings.

*

Observation.

Quantity says nothing to the mind, but everything to the senses. Nothing to the mind; the geometer ignores and swallows it in the forms he fathers.

But the senses, but the ear, the eye, the feeling spirit, are aroused, exalted, crushed by this endlessness of repetition.

The mind abhors the innumerable, and look! for a whole day now the waves about to die have been saluting it....

A REMARKABLE OCCURRENCE

September 26th.

Sunset. Clear sky, the orange disk exactly tangent to the watery horizon.

Those on the beach keep silence without knowing why, a three-minute silence.

Solemnity of this passing. The sense of a beheading in the involved depths of these minutes. The day's head slowly tumbles.

The disk is swallowed. When it has quite gone a child cries *All over*! Everyone seems shaken to have seen *one of his own days executed in front of him.*

For a little while the vestiges of this prodigious happening persist on my retina. I am strangely moved by the sense of necessity, the inevitable, the inflexible clock, the precision of the forces of inertia.

The strange situation of mortals; the enormous inequalities of size, the differences of nature and duration, suddenly *visible* between the two protagonists who compose the instant; the immediate sensation of a formidable hierarchy of importance: all weigh upon thought and impress upon it for a time their images, as those that are too dazzling persist, then fade in the eye, by degrees of complementary colors. Thus thought responds, or seems to respond, to these too mighty visions of "nature" with replicas that are nobly pale, according to the ordinary principles of contrast. It invokes its own ability, the transcendence of its own faculty of knowing, quite heedless of the naïve automatism of its retorts. To advance the *contrary* suffices as a defense; but no more than suffices.

And certainly thought has to defend itself against the contemplation of such visions. Its length of life and awareness wholly subject to the vagaries of the body; its existence and death sweeping like a revolving star over a telescope's fixed field; its extinction seen and inflicted as a direct and minimal consequence of the exigencies of the clock; all human things disparaged, depreciated, brought to nothing by the brushing of a star against the soul, a unilateral dependence. . . . I leave my sentence hanging. For this is precisely what I have wished to make clear, that such *propositions* admit no *riders*.

Now the sea seems to carry a whole green-violet glassware leaping and chopping. The child of a moment ago is now devouring a sandy crust that I feel between my own teeth grating.

*

Sands.

Of the open sea.

 Atlantic.

The great swell traveling from America with its splendid hollow and untroubled rondure runs at last upon shelf, scarp, and bar.

The molecule bursts its chain. The white horses overleap themselves.

Here the foam builds long-enduring stranded rafts that offer little iridescent walls of dirty breaking bubbles to the beach-mark of the so far highest wave.

The wind carves cats and sheep of this material and puffs them bowling comically, as if terrified of the sea, toward the dunes. This foam is not whipped water but a messy frothing of silica and salt.

But the fresh virgin foam is of a strange softness to the feet. It is a gassy, sparkling, lukewarm milk that comes at you with a voluptuous rush, swamping your feet, your ankles, washing them, giving them to drink, then subsiding, retiring from the margin with a voice of farewell while your statue settles a little deeper into the drift and your soul, borne by this vast yet infinitely delicate music, is calmed and carried with it away.

*

The same.

High sea at Mer Sauvage. Never were waves higher, heavier, more worked or working; never more foaming. At the water's edge a barrier of congealed foam persists along the tidemark, from which the wind tears off big cat-sized lumps and bowls them up the slope of hard sand and on toward the dunes. They look like animals. This aerated jelly is bloated, yellowish, gluey, formed of silica and salt water.

Crushing effect of this indefinitely prolonged bombardment. The seeming convulsion goes on, inexhaustible. Boredom, sleep, induced by this wonderful inorganic action, apparent anger, lifting and crashing of dead things, insurrection of the inert.

*

Rocks.

Some black; some silvery; some flesh-pink.

Some shining and squared, with blunt soft edges. Others with sharp clean cracks or thick and jagged laminations. Some shapeless, some large. Some look as individual as people. To each its nature, its form, its history. Indeed its form *is* its history.

I progress through this chaos to sea-noises.

A strange dance, or perhaps *precisely the opposite* of a dance, this walk that is governed by a terrain without laws. The body can foresee nothing, each step is a new invention of the moment and the eye. No step resembles another, none has the stretch, the contour, the dynamic of the one before. Nothing is custom. There is no distance set between slave and master. Just as, in times of stress, the powers and the people cling together.

Nevertheless I do observe some kind of rhythm for, through all the ups and downs, the irregular succession of leaps and clamberings, I try to maintain an average momentum. In this country of jumbled staircases, it is both hard and good to travel. All the muscles work, and work extempore; at every moment the center must invent the posture of its man, allotting its energies anew.

A highly complex game of chess is being played; at every move the problem alters. The pieces are the images which the eye takes in, Euclidean calculations of displacement, the various independent groupings of muscles, and many things besides.

Any thought which is not simply, *How reach the sea*, or bearing upon that, and which cannot be translated in terms of economy of forces or prevision of efforts, is as if canceled or nipped in the bud. Such is the player intent on his game.

And now these calculations of the nerves and skeleton draw near their term. I see the foam between enormous altars, huge dice, and upturned tables.

*

Swimming.

I seem to refind myself and to reknow myself when I return to this universal water. I know nothing of crops or vintages. Nothing in the Georgics for me.

But to throw oneself into the burly of mass and movement, to labor at one's uttermost, and from neck to toes; to toss in this pure deep element; to drink and breathe the sacred sharpness—all this is for me a game like the game of love, an act in which my whole body is compact of deeds and signals, like a hand that opens, closes, speaks, performs. All the frame gives itself here, withdraws itself, conceives itself, then spends itself to the last exhaustion of the possible. It embraces *her*, would seize *her*, hug *her*, becomes mad with life and with *her* loves light mobility, possesses *her*, fathers upon *her* a thousand strange conceptions. Through her I am that man I would be. My body becomes the immediate tool of the mind and yet at the same time the author of all the mind's ideas. All grows clear for me. *I know utterly what love could be.* Excess of the real! Knowledge is caresses. The lover's deeds are the patterns of works of art.

So *swim*! and plunge your head into this wave that rolls toward you, with you, then breaks and knocks you down!

*

For a few moments I thought that I should never escape from the sea. It cast me forth, then sucked me back in its indomitable windings. The withdrawal of the huge billow that had coughed me up upon the sand swallowed the sand back with me. In vain I thrust my arms into this sand, it sank with all my body. As I still struggled feebly, an even mightier billow chucked me up like jetsam upon the golden margin of no-man's-land.

I walk finally upon the immense beach, shivering and drinking the wind. It buffets from the southwest, catching the waves crossways, brushing and bruising them, crisping and scaling them with a network of secondary ripples that they carry with them all the way from the horizon to the final bar upon which they shatter in foam.

A happy barefoot man, I walk drunk with walking upon a mirror ceaselessly polished by an infinitely thin slice of sea.

*

Psalm.

Free walking sings unaided. Impossible not to create whilst walking. To create whilst walking is as simple and natural as maintaining the seemingly free rhythms of the limbs. One has not to *fix* these private creations. Yet I have fixed this one, and a few others, to serve me as memorials.

WHEN AS UPON THE SEABOARD

When as upon the seaboard
Between the two elements
On the pendulum tidemark
The wave gives and ungives,
Lashes and spreads,
Retches and swallows,

Delivers, and repents,
Touches, tumbles, groans, embraces
And to the mass returns
And into the mother returns,
Eternal revision,
I on the struck forehead of the ocean
Founder between two sheets of water. . . .
Hour of regretting
That is ended, endless. . . .
What does that hour enclose?
What's bridled in, what's swallowed back?
What's measured me, out-held, then snatched away?
Your overwhelming impotence, O Wave,
Ever to issue or to leap quite clear!
Your every act contains its own annulling
As down you go, not free
To disrupt the embodied economy of sea.
Sea you remain and not to be stilled
But must subside with mournful rattle,
Contracted gathered and confounded
In her the numberless and unbounded,
As notion into body returns,
As thought falls back
From the point to which her secret cause
Had dared to lift her and cannot hinder
Her strict reversion into everything
That is not she, this she that is not she
Nor this long time has been, nor had the time
Either to disconnect herself from all
Or to begin again, again to begin. . . .
This will be always for another time,
For the next time and for the time after

On the sea-border,
To an infinity of times
And times' disorder.

*

Hearken continually, attend
To the chant of waiting and the brunt of weathers,
To the long lulling of her quantity,
Her reckonings, her identity,
Bold boastful shadow's voice,
Tremendous voice, the sea's,
Saying and saying "I gain, I lose,
I lose, I gain," dull rhyme.
O ! out of time to snatch a time !

*

Lonelier than lonely by the seaboard
Wave I become, and try
The droning alchemy that alters
The waters into the waters
And I into I.

*

Pilgrimage.
Chapel in the island of C.

... these inmost depths of the church where something obscure is occurring. A mystery, or a silliness: nothing, or a miracle.

I feel an *other* invade me. I am seized with a primitive shudder. There is a breath on my skin, an illusory horror enwraps me, a prickling into zones of heat and cold.

The priest with the pyx, carrying from mouth to mouth the sustenance of an enigma, puts me inescapably in mind of a huge golden insect mechanically fertilizing rows of females that are continuously replaced. With a little winking shaking flame he visits these dark settled forms, that doubtless open at the moment of his passing, receive, and close again. The operculum shut, each founders, dwindles and is as dead —they gather themselves and make their way home, altered, hooded, absorbed. They make their way home silent, concentrated, eyes down, each with her private secret that is nevertheless the same for all.

All made one, turned in upon themselves. I think of that primitive marine animal that can turn itself inside-out like a glove.

Then of what is this the *reflex*?

What is the pattern behind the detail, what are the shapes, durations, physical connections of this sacred horror and inwardness?

For I observe myself and feel as it were a freshening wave break over my shoulders, as though I were a reef on which the swell runs headlong, declaring itself in whiteness and sound. I note it as over my flesh it rises, is there, and then subsides. From it I derive no notions, nor do I seek to oppose or to attach to it ideas. It is a *fact*. For myself, a *fact without connections*. . . . Is this then "refusing grace"?

Is this then Grace, Spirit, the inward Visitant? Or is it a complex effect of silence and shadows, of a present place and moment wholly interpenetrated by the past?

I leave. An abrupt consortium of fogs veils all beyond the pointed rock-heads of the foreground.

All (I think) that is affective is obtuse. The affective is what reaches us by elementary channels, through organs lacking the delicacies and multiple *co-ordinations* of the specialized organs of the senses.

Yet we attempt to compare these crude *values*, powerful but blurred, with the clear informations of organized perception. And we cannot manage it but are like geometers faced with irrational and transcendent grandeurs, vainly essaying to convert to finite numbers a continuum.

Psalm on a Voice

Under the breath
Of a soft small voice speaking greatly
Of large, surprising, deep, and accurate matters
In a voice that is soft and small.
Menace of thunder, presence of absolutes,
In a voice of robin,
In a delicacy of essential sound, a flute's precision.
And the whole sun adumbrated
Between the lips of a smile.
(O under-breath)
And of the nature of a murmur
In a French infinitely pure.
If you couldn't catch the words, if you heard them at
  a distance,
You would have thought "a voice saying nothings."
And they were nothings for
An ear at ease.
But this contrast, music, this voice
Barely ruffling the air,
This whispered power,
These perspectives, gulfs, foretold maneuvers,
  discoveries,

This smile dismissing the universe ! ...

I think also finally
Of the silk-noise, alone and discreet,
Of a fire creating a whole room
By a self-devouring.
It speaks to itself.
Or, almost for its own sake,
It speaks to me.

In the Square

IN THE SQUARE a Man sat comfortably, giving bread or grain to the pigeons. A whole gray-blue nation crowding at his feet, over his feet, onto his hands, his shoulders; they covered him, fanned him, pecked and billed him even to his beard.

A Man leaning upon a stick gazed fixedly upon this scene. He could not remove his eyes from it.

A Man said to him: "That's a long time you've been there! It's always the same thing, other people give it a glance and go."

The Man with the stick answered him without moving: "Be quiet! I have no time for pigeons. I am observing myself observing. I hear what speaks to me, or what speaks to itself, in what I see.

"The grain attracts the pigeons. The pigeons attract the eye. This eye *pecks*, *bills*, *corners*. This eye *murmurs*, *sketches*, *expresses*—vaguely, confusedly.

"And this creates a second spectacle; and that creates a second spectator. It makes me a second-hand witness, and that is *the final* thing. There is no witnessing at third hand, for I am incapable of constructing some Someone who should see *from further on*, who should see what *he* sees-and-does who sees *him-who-is-seeing-the-pigeons*.

"Thus I stand at the terminus of some capacity, for there is now no more room in my mind for a little more mind."

The Man without a stick shrugged his shoulders, and made off quickly, shrugging them still.

He carried some sort of encumbrance in his head, arising from what he had just heard; something that he could neither conceive nor forget.

The Old Woman

VERY ANCIENT, I inhabit the world between worlds, already almost at a point of rest in regard to acts and moments, like a body without life.

I touch you and I am far from you. We share an instant but it bears very different meanings for you and for me. My memory is a house quite built: an enchanted house that might vanish in a winking, as it has always been since the moment came when there was absolutely nothing more to add. All possible projects have been accomplished or abandoned. I have only one fresh deed to do. All is done, all is redone, but death only.

I am touchy about light, noise, flavors, nourishment. All that comes to me now comes either too well known or unknowable.

II

On the old woman's face with the troubled eyes, the beat of the four-square music evokes a childish interest, a feeble attention, a baby's smile—as if this rhythm of unachieved dance had picked up in the tangled skein, in the labyrinth of eighty winters, a few threads not yet followed, not yet played out, idle since infancy; something to occupy her, something to *learn*, to make beginnings over, still move with the moving world.

Novelty permits a certain rejuvenation.

Miniatures

Miniatures

THE YOUNG MOTHER

THIS AFTERNOON of highest summer is as round as an orange at the climax of its term.

The whole growingness of the garden, the light, life itself, cross gently through the epochs of their perfection. It seems that all things, from their very origin, have worked only toward this transient brilliant ripening. Happiness shines like the sun.

It is the purest of her own substance that glows in the cheeks of the child that the young mother holds. She hugs him to her, that he will be always herself.

She clasps what she has made. She forgets, yet rejoices, that she has given herself, for she recovers and discovers herself unendingly in the soft touch of this skin whose coolness makes her drunk. In vain her white hands cup the fruit that she has grown, she cannot feel herself other than quite pure, a virgin crowned.

Absently her eyes brush over the flowers and branches, the splendid ensemble of the world.

She is like a natural philosopher who has found his master-notion, and made what he must.

She cannot decide whether the center of the universe is in

her own heart or in that little heart that beats in her arms, giving life to everything.

THE FLYING MAN

In the impossible, in what his nature forbids, lies endless temptation for man. He can think of nothing more awful than living as himself. He envies the fishes' freedom in their sea games, sporting in the depths as easily as they frolic at the water's skin.

Still more do we envy such creatures as have been given the liberties of the air. How happy they seem there ! And yet it is their necessity that is our caprice. It is their daily toiling that is the very model of our dreams.

And now we have at last succeeded in turning ourselves into flying animals. We have built machines of wood and canvas. We fix to them a jet of wind that puffs them up to the top of the sky, in the thinnest of thin air, far above all clouds. Death is our passenger. She accompanies us into the sun, over the waving arms of the sea, across the map. She looks at Paris as though she had spat it out. But so overweening is she, so intoxicated with her splendid opportunities, that she cuts a poor figure beside the flying driver, who pays her no attention.

This scorn is his true engine.

THE HUNTRESS

The huntress wearies.

Suddenly she must lean against a trunk, she must think.

Fatigue confuses and breaks off the chase. The body commands, the quarry vanishes. A girl all scarlet and panting abandons pursuit; her momentum subsides into things gone, things to come.

Now she is powerless the stag comes gazing at her with pity: he stretches his moist muzzle toward her breast, that rises and falls.

Little by little the whole of legend draws near to the stranded huntress, comes down from limbs and clouds, ventures from covert. One sniffs at her gaiters, another licks the hand of this spent mortal who has yielded to the eternities of the forest. They peck her earlobes.

The whole of legend and the whole of childhood approach reassured, melting into each other, by grace of the shades and crossroads of this mysterious repose, compound of weariness, of memories, and the vague deep murmuring of life or the wood.

AT THE RACES

Elixir emerges. At once he is garlanded with thousands of images of himself. He is in a hundred thousand hearts; each sees him victor or vanquished.

His steps on the clean grass radiate the importance with

which they are invested. He is well aware that he will shortly have to burn himself up almost. In a few moments, for a few moments, he will shine out beyond all the horses of the world. For five minutes he must put forth the impossible utmost of his power. Nothing exists on the far side of that fire. There is no future.

The ears and nostrils of Elixir prematurely sense the *Off*! His whole skin is infinitely awake. Already he gulps the air as though he would breathe in some larger soul capable of an eternal energy. His nobly unadulterate blood is pulsing with hope and pride.

His breeding, his strangely fine-drawn form, his mantle which is of sunlight and shiverings alone, make him a monster of brilliancy and elegance.

Irene, arrayed in her rouge, blue eyes, and pearls, cannot compete with the frothing favorite in this matter of beauty. I lay no bet on her.

Dazzling beast! On golden pasterns he prances with force and presence. But his heart is already running.

DANCE

Life, why is it not one long Dance? How do we manage to get on without an endless harmony between our acts and their durations? Are we not linked chains of our successive postures that emerge from one another, matching and counterbalancing each other?

Do you not agree that whatever cannot be done dancing is brutish?

Suppose all our lives were subjected to the noble and supple disciplines of the ballet—imagine ! Eating, speaking, walking, breathing in tempo.

The moment music inspires us we are creatures of another planet.

Give me your hand. Let us enter the temple of our acts. Let us enter by way of rhythm into vitality and live this night like gods !

It grows late, do you say? True, and one by one night strips herself of all these dancing forms that tire themselves to sleep. They go out like stars.

But we, we have yet to drain these last drops of the energy that bears us onward only into dawn; for we have trodden down all the hours of love. . . .

AMAZON

Mare, my good mare, let us go into the forest and think only of ourselves ! The sharp air, shadows, trees, the shying, the movements of your movement: the phantoms the gallop plucks furiously from the twiggage, then tosses away behind: the long deep landscapes that your course half opens, then slams shut again: and those strange revolving defiles piercing the innumerable columns of the woods as one races through —let them waft our spirits into the dizzy absence of a dream !

And your body shall bear my body. I am beautiful as you are beautiful. You are mine and I yours. . . . Off we go, hop !

No, wait an instant whilst I fix my cap, whilst I pin on my breast this red and solid rose, whilst I take from the groom this crop with the slender lash.

It is not for you, my yellow-haired beast. It is for young men who dare not take love lightly.

THE PIANO AND THE SONG

A strange marriage, this of the vibrant voice to the abstract voice of the piano. The breath of her of the red hair, the hands of her of the brown, move both worlds, of the temporal and the physical.

The room vibrates. The walls sing. The air, its substance shaken by a young strong throat, fragmented by ten thousand crystal shocks from the mighty percussions of the steel wires struck, becomes the seat of miraculous transformations. Successively my stretched-out soul receives every impress that even life could ordain it.

I shudder, I sense a force of the unknown. I am sunk in melancholy, I endure all the melancholy and the lacerations of a tenderness, in solitude. Listen again! Here are the trappings of expectation: here is anguish to the life.

This sustained bass touches the secret depths of one's being. This movement is a slumber in a wood. This startling resolution sketches a whole philosophy, which will never become articulate.

An infinite love passes by like a leaf twisting and turning....

"Ah, what a voice, my child!"

"Dear lady, you accompany so well!"

All my powers descend to earth. They feel heavy and clumsy. Language is abashed.

FINERY

A finished woman must be capable of three things: of seduction, of infatuation, of production. With these, she is perfect.

It is a woman's body that ties the knot of her destiny. But this flesh that owes it to itself to be moving, moved, fecund, has often to call upon intelligence to get there. Nature does not always make her handiwork as desirable as she should.

Now custom, and for that matter climate, demand that this flesh should be veiled, enveloped. Instinct frets at it. Intelligence takes a hand. Art is born.

All these garments obscure from us this body whose sweetness and softness are so important; yet art sets out to construct from them the most insidious sleights in the strategy of the nude.

Through choice of material, fineness of stuffs, charm of line; by means of the delicate play between what one exposes to the gazer and what one denies: a body (which is, after all, so simple and straightforward a thing) becomes a metaphysical object. Our unreason reasons: All that has value is guarded, therefore all that is guarded has value.

Women, women, you must please! If not, the world ends.

THE HOLDUP

We want money. We get it where it is to be got. We like neither work nor insecurity. We do not drudge and we do not gamble. We shall buy revolvers and silk masks—or a woman's stocking will do. In the secrecy of a coppice we shall lay our plans; in a café we shall study the railway timetable. We shall take this smart night train. It is full of the rich asleep. We know that at such-and-such a point it will go slow. There we shall station our friends with the stolen car. We two shall wait, and at the proper hour you will get up from your seat. I shall keep guard in the corridor, a six-shooter in either hand. Abruptly you will switch on the light. Abruptly you will make the grand entry that freezes limbs and hearts. We need kill only the brave. . . .

There is a good deal of calculation and risk in this affair. There are miserable types who hand over phony wallets—there isn't time to count up. Then there are the terrifying wheels of the train that we jump from. There are the man hunts through the fields, the snares laid in the shadows. At first dawn a cigarette falls from numb lips and there is a man like any other, whose thumb is already on the button of the alarm.

JUNK

A bust. A bedstead. A lampshade, a School Geometry. All these things that a man has managed to acquire for his use are taken away from him in the end by the onward movement of the world.

He tires of them: or he dies: or he grows poor. Or sometimes it is riches that come, and still his goods are stripped from him, for now he finds them insufficiently grand.

All round the clock the junkman strikes. The hour of the thousand partings comes to all poor pieces in the end. Here is furniture that is stateless, ornaments that are orphans, sad books that have lost their souls.

They unsettle into chaos, they jostle without recognition.

They are no longer useful, pleasing, protected by familial gods. Outrages ensue, a clock in a washbasin, a saucepan cocked against a mirror admires its own reflection.

Poor things! Some will spend two months in these infernal regions: others are in for half a century.

But in the end the fancier always comes. Even this cracked jug is not without some hope of resurrection. Notions will have changed and it will go to the Louvre.

AN INTERIOR

Irene is a pauper: she can see the walls through her threadbare thoughts. This lady's soul can provide no furnishings for the apartment in which she sits.

Her thirty-two millions must come to her help. They run to the shops, they turn into lacquer and marquetry. They levy tribute from China, and all the holy places. Here are Venice, Versailles; here are Beauvais, Smyrna, Persia, Coromandel. Nothing is too beautiful to serve as screen between the soul of Irene and the image of her nothingness. The world must encompass her about with all that is found in it of most delight; the creations of art obey the injunctions of her inexhaustible balance at the bank.

Her neighbor is a man who needs no other scenery than a grate. Or he stares into the blankness of his sheet of paper, or at an imaginary point in space.

THE SCREEN

On the taut cloth, on the ever virgin rectangle where neither life nor blood itself leaves traces, the most complicated events work themselves out as often as one wills.

Actions are speeded up or slowed down. Their order may be reversed. The dead revive and laugh.

Everyone can see with his own eyes that all that is, is surface.

From everyday life that part of it is extracted that was light. This comes and comes again in the midst of darkness. We can watch the precision of the real assuming the attributes of the dream.

It is an artificial dream. It is, too, an external memory, endowed with mechanical perfection. Finally, by means of stills and close-ups, the act of attention is itself represented.

My spirit is split by these illusions.

It gazes at the busy all-powerful screen. It shares the passions of the ghosts born there. It is impregnated with their acts—the way this one smiles, that one declares his passion; the way to get over a wall; the way to kill; the way to ponder visibly....

But the other effect of these images is the more strange. This facility is a criticism of life. What are they going to be worth, these acts and deeds whose interchanges I witness in all their monotonous diversity? I have no more mind to live, for it is no longer anything but copying. I know the future by heart.

Early Pieces

Agatha

THE MORE I think, the more I think; yes, ever newer I see all known things within me become astonishing, and afterward still more known. Suddenly I have slowly conceived them: when they vanish, they do it easily.

I am changing in shadow, in a bed. An idea that has lost its beginning becomes clear but false, but pure, then empty or huge or old: it becomes even nothing, and so rises to the unexpected, bringing with it my whole mind.

My body is scarcely aware that the indistinct and easy volumes of the bed support it; upon it, my sovereign flesh regards and stirs the darkness. I fix, disturb, and lose by the movement of my eyes, some center in lightless space; and nothing in the black tableau shifts.

The result is that a glimmer quite close to me is born.

On the nakedness or velvet of midnight or the mind, this dubious tardy feeble effort is all that is left of the bright clarity that went before; no more than adequate, it maintains amidst the busy shade an exiguous remnant of the glittering day—day thought of, and thinking almost. This paltry glimmer resolves into a dull and fleeting cheek, a pointless face soon smiling against me, responsive, itself consumed by luster-swallowing dusk.

It is my depth I touch. To such a succession of self-generated forms all invention returns, whether it be a matter of the rebirth, here, far from all scales of comparison, after an indeterminable interval of pursuing his private paths, forever unknowable, of *the being who is made for oblivion*; or whether it is a return of scattered magical diurnal fragments, the constellation of the forms of common daylight now wholly dismantled.

The darkness fathers forth a few scraps still, of a flimsy seascape, ruffles them, and the icy crupper of a horse. . . . My continuancy softly pursues the methodical destruction of a whole series of foci of this sort, necessary in an annihilated domain.

Upon this sophistical shadow I scrawl, as if with phosphorus, the fading formulas I need; and when I reach the end, near the point of their resumption, I must always trace them out again, for the more I nourish them the deeper they sleep, before I come to change them. Yes, but once I have hurried and harried them to their deaths I disdain plodding and tracing and distributed emphasis, I release within me a wellhead of perfect agility, reviving every physical nuance, unwind the action of swimming with wet eyes, abundance of flexible indolence with feet floating in the fullness of high water. . . . Human, almost upright in the coiled spring of the sea, swathed in enormous cold, upon whom the whole hugeness weighs, even to his shoulders, even to his ears despoiled of variable noise, I still touch the strange absence of soil, as if a ground of notions altogether new; and with the last scraps of my strength I tremble. My powers are unhinged, my feebleness not what it was. This incomprehensible facility oversets me, troubling, absorbing, the whole workings of my frame.

Yet icier deeps, concealed below, forgo me but will mount again to drink me in some dream.

It costs me nothing, the being possessed by these abysses, profound enough but perishable, for I feel their forces only in intervals between two periods of knowing my own. To the huge calm about me I reply with acts enlarged into veritable monsters of moving and changing. Who can this be who in repose happily overturns and disengages? Who sports and circles unaccustomed, unorigined and unnamed? WHO is asking? The same who replies. The same who writes, effacing a same line. They are but writings on water.

Once my powers are deluded, I possess them more than ever.

At this hour that is not an hour, who cares for my history? I despise it like a book. For this is the ideal chance: to strip all mortal order of memory, annul my experience, illumine what was inapposite and, by a mere night dream, to escape so free that I no longer recognize even my own body. All seems partial. In this amplitude I steer my spirit toward chance and, in no wise like a sleeper, surrender myself in absolute clarity.

And now, already, all transformations are visible, and certainty infinite because infinitely divided. All serious sentiments display a common death. Gone is the unbroken watchfulness of the thread of awareness; no longer do I hear the endless murmur of the profound inexhaustible sibyl who calculates each particle of approaching futurity, who mysteriously sums the elements of duration: to the last known the first unknown, without fault or looking backward—a foreseeing ever flowing, launching into the fatal new from the intimate consequence of every instant, casting over the ensemble of unforced days a semblance of lucidity by her imperceptible preparation for their alterations. Now I experience no more cruxes of the within. All proceeds unamazedly, the springs of surprise run down. The most disparate entities embrace without that contact making me extraordinary. Comprehension has no prey and no peculiar solidity distinguishes particular notions.

This drift, different from dream, admits me close enough to the desired secrets of sleep, were it not that—slight and blurred, into that unique compound where my usual beings devour one another indifferently—something extraneous enters: a noise, or waves enveloping the distance. In the offing fades away, unless I reanimate it, an imposing mass of mud and fires.

The tail-end of the town-noises penetrates my private sphere. It is the moment when all grows still and echoes thin away. The last changes are reckoned. An inordinate exterior region divests itself of existence.

Hearing expands; to the very horizon, and it overhangs a gulf that grows immense. A continually more subtle creature leans over the void to catch the slightest sound; through her I plumb a space where the possible breathes and I fly! as no sound quenches the desire for sound, to the limit of my own sustention—to the dinning of my blood and the animation of my enduring moment.

So still the silence and so strong the night, they wake me deeper and deeper.

How pure the will to tomorrow, the road I take to tomorrow! I feel uncertainty speed from the forehead of time, the event arrive, its vigor, its languor, the dissolution of experience, and the rebirth of the voyage, as pure and hard as itself, adorned in unending mind. The new sheds itself in advance, by way of a shift more imperceptible than the angle of the sky....

You can only know yourself in reverse. You carry *backward* a power, a kind of discernment; and, being able to see only the opposite way to the one you travel, you analyze what is finished, you act out only what is done already.

Once, I would reflect upon a magnificent number of subjects; but now I am so peaceful that I seem to myself as if set apart, and suspended between this finite number and another whole mass, imminent but probably not in any connection with it. Each problem is drawn in these two different directions so that the intervening space acts as a sort of natural form of interrogation. All that I know attracts toward it all that I do not know; but whenever I think to unite, in the midst of the tenebrous region, ideas that I still possess in their distinctness, I recall that I may well corrupt all the evidence, darkening what I will, and not necessarily lightening what I will. There is always more than one escape-way from my certainty.

The quality of this calm is so limpid that if I am edged for a few moments around the same thought, I infer, from their mere diversity, this very thought; I see how it happens, I predict its returns, I play with the power of snapping it off sharp and, when it is thus broken, simulating for it a certain beginning.

Or else, I advance along an idea up to a known limit to which rigorous thinking always leads me no matter from where I begin, and surrender myself to difficulty unadorned —which, incapable of further self-metamorphosis, still pure, by being immovable leaves me to be invaded by the residual music of my mind. I have seemed to linger about the rim of an impenetrable circle within which I feel sure that there is something that would provide me long enjoyment: something brief, universal: an abstract, imminent pearl would roll into a deep fold of common thought: an astonishing law, cosubstantial with its seeker, would inhabit there: work of a moment to get this pearl free: a few words would fix it forever.

Whether it be a great brightness, always in the tail of the eye, or a being as inviolate as the center of an orbit, its dwelling yields neither image nor doubt. Off all tracks, inaccessible to all assaults, it lies buried in simple certitude outside all metaphor and resemblance; as a boulder is motionless to a train of living fingers.

Of it I possess the desire; the suspicion; the approximate location; the consequences: only the fancied ones. Neither its form nor its powers—but of these I discover endlessly everything that they are not, and of this lack I have made a working symbol.

At times, relinquishing the search, I pretend that I have found, and happily manipulate the in fact not yet true: within myself I shuffle the numberless permutations of meditation, and I prophesy; for a sort of flimsy response, visibly fragile, accompanies problems at the moment of their appearance—they never manifest themselves unallied with a winged provisional solution, where the sense of the true begins.

Determine the effects of some entity exceedingly desired by the mind: once seen, it would ingest into its own splendid immutability every thought capable of pursuing it; so that the powers of new invention would grow enfeebled. In the first place it would be so entirely satisfying that only the greatest *distraction* could be directly substituted for it: I should know that we would meet again. It's all in the game; I win, I lose, and there's a connection. . . .

Now I am near perhaps, on the verge of laws: in this unblemished nocturnal envelope, where every thought undergoes self-modulation, turns back for self-observation, trailing a latency, and where the dark and delicate unity of my senses, all equally desert, appears so easily extended that the profoundest deductions, the most interior penetrations, accomplish themselves in the sight of my whole watchful powers in a single indistinguishable limpidity. *If* there could always be this purity, removing the complete execution of a thought from contingency, permitting the separation of its aspects and the division of the intellectual continuum into clearly defined intervals—I should very soon make all my ideas irreducible or compounded.

So still I preserve the variety of my unease: I maintain a disorder within me the better to attract my own powers or whatever dispersion awaits them.

And since, voluptuously, the palpitation of multiple space scarcely animates my flesh any more; and I no longer willingly taste any idea in isolation. The assemblage of diverse modes of knowing, all equally in prospect, by which I am constituted, governed, foretold from on high, by the sense of my own antiquity, now forms a system quite null and indifferent to what it might produce or fathom, when the fancied shadow softly yields to utter birth, and it is mind—unless still, all very strange, very solitary at the outer edge of this universe, a doubt, a hint, a breath, all of them unique, occasionally interchange.

At this point, above the calm, shines the fact that *relevance* is master of the world, the binding of the idea to the point of its apparition.

An idea rises of itself and takes the place of another: none among them can be more important than its hour.

They ascend, original; in a meaningless order; mysteriously moved toward the admirable noon of my presence, where burns, as it best may, the sole thing that exists: the any *one*.

Thus too their whole natural quantity: one among them.

Pure Dramas

The scene is set about with modest jewels that gleam.

If, in silence, in sun, in shade, the Earth turns in her mighty slumber, a flash of brooches illustrates that dusky gesture.

Flying foam—venturesome clouds grazed by a quill (with water drops) in the water reflecting them—winged hands sleeved in reeds, limpid hands, their bee's or star's desire to pilfer fluttering their calyxes open, shut, but catching only a little thin sky—and, gems— and, between the stalks, long by bounty of the radiant rains, the gentle human form sometimes, foot-free . . . all lovely debris of a truth demolished by a thunderbolt, the morning Poet singles them, gilding them with the luster of an eye that is pure.

(Eye whose virtues of childhood would be fleeting, did not at each dawn trickle down its mirror, sprung from some smiling false- hood, a discreet ichor of tears.)

Antique ambition—to resuscitate the spectacle, angelic once, now damned, of these nakednesses enjoying life *! One must love them taken unawares in a celestial puddle whose thin ice apes absolute ether, or thinks it lucidly.*

Let us indulge our hour of these precious Beings—since there is no longer a Theater to amuse the shades—and no one *to enter upon the threshold of this Plato's cave, under a flare grown already ideal.*

Out of a clump of sensitive rushes, head of vegetable hair buzzing with insects, springs in the golden motes, nameless jewel, enigmatic, alone, a rosy arm that flowers in a sleeping hand whose white fingers scarcely stir, moved by some pleasure under the green, or by some vague desire, or by the breeze.

Over the speechless mouths of a red crowd of corollas, scarcely moving them in their aimless course, come pure Feet, lower ornaments of one mere couple otherwise unseen, of whom one flees the other, the girl. I will have the flowers in silhouettes and the limbs swift; the great toe drawn somewhat after a spiral.

A hand of water (behind it one sees the sea-green morning) is stretched out, and its first two fingers, extended alone, offer to the east a frail jewel, a stalk whose terminal butterfly quivers its wings, desiring a falling forever into the void that films it blue—sweet-smelling snow.

No longer trembling in the cup harmoniously worn by the long rains on the rock, into the chalice of the sky evaporates cold water of dew, a cloud.

The great light disburdens it.

And thus the dawn of forms.

Perhaps it wakes in order to invent shame ... to hide its riches under a crook'd arm? Do I know?

But—quite simply—it is a cloud.

These holy moths, regardless soon of all the gay tufts shining in the mullioned light, fill me with fear for the landscape. One feels that all the trembling garden will take flight —and, if the minute's flowers sport wings to flee with, where shall we go, Ideas?

... It poises on the calyxes, it winks through petals, this little magic lamp. Ah, what a night !—to seize it, cradle it in the hollow of childish hands, to run, and laugh to have it captive—a Star!

All these images are still adulterated by the implacable certitude of their elements. Solitary harmony offers to the self-intoxicated soul a more delicious liberty. It is only pure lines that make the hard-headed artist weep, without remorse. Impurity! to desire a grimace or the brutality of cries. Nothing counts but divination and death.

Then praise the pure Drama of a line drawn upon heaven-colored or upon life-colored space! Only in beautiful movement can it exist. It is the surest of all things, the ornament of every life. Divine it! It eternizes the centuries of the smile, and then it droops in melancholy, then knots itself or draws its spiral tight—or it dreams; now spins away, abandoned in joy to flying upward, curves back (habit or memory), and there beyond all stars encounters Another, ferried by unknown fates to a like East, and will never be done with flowering, vanishing into the wonder of the game—charmed, diverse, monotonous—flimsy and black.

The Old Alleys

MUSTY DUSK, burdened with cellars' breathings of thick cold; heavy slumbers of the old alleys; you set me dreaming shadowy dreams.

Leaving the peopled squares, the swarming of life, heady with food smells, bright with the copper of pots, lulled by the drip and sparkle of fountained water, I love your moist shades and great black walls pierced by tall and blacker windows, upon the spiny twistings of whose rusty grilles spiders hang out blue sails, gray sails, to the airs. . . .

. . . Disquieting cats are crouched in the obscure, while others mew and prowl.

Scraps of blue sky at corners, and the sun tosses a handful of bright sovereigns onto a flagstone. The houses are blind and deaf: down their walls trail ropes of sickly vegetation from the scorched tiles above, and they are spattered with bony efflorescences, gangrenes, cankers, swelling the beams, bubbling the plaster, crumbling the pitted stones. . . . A vast abandon hangs over all. And questionable creatures creep there, gnaw and rot.

. . . And all this dumb despair, this victory of the toadstool, scorpion, rat, this triumph of Death and Ruin, put one in mind of the unrecorded crimes hidden in these bowels of masonry, of the men fatally attracted into the Night . . . and

of tubs of guts swilled by swine, and of monstrous Jew-dives;
and every door appears to guard a mystery and every paving
stone to sweat with old spilled blood; and the yowling of the
furious cats and uneasy cackling of invisible hens evoke mass
murders of little children, a lurid gleam that lights a trembling
blade, that plays in a murky courtyard over faces yellow and
drawn, and filthy scarlet rendezvous!...

Unpublished Pages

(*Fragment*)

I WAKE, and yawn at creation. Art is a child's game. Science is dreary and clumsy, the Apple has the worm. No! nothing is complex, distant, truly secret, or subtle.... Quite pretty, though, that indistinct rain-patter tapping the weary leaves. That, and that alone. The world is as ridiculous as a wagging clock. Fools of stars are spinning, a few, neither beautiful, finally, nor awe-inspiring. And what are they to me, such silly human skulls!... These types who let their hair grow and stand profiled against heaven like Orpheuses, lyres into the blue and eyes upturned—because they can take a six-footed line and break its back in the middle, or muster a crowd of identical consonants. Disgusting!... Flowers are as crass as women. And vice versa too. Architecture—a widow! Slim volumes—we are the ones who perpetrate them, forsooth... let us find one and ink it over. More, one cannot even drink anything that does not taste stupid. Only one scent is aesthetically pleasing, salt: and coal, a little! Incense stinks. Death gets an awful bore. Explosion is the only way to end, that or a five-master plummeting in open sea.

Language is bankrupt. Nature... grows pot-bellied. The other world does not exist. The pagans are stupid: the Christians, quite terrifyingly ugly. Hamlet would be all right if there were not that play all round him. The scientists stink of the parvenu!... Oh, science! Alas, they want to abolish mystery....

...Romanticism! Ah no, my soul!... Or rather, yes! Causes and effects, gentlemen, are without reality.... Style! A bore: I see it under construction like a mosaic, dully contrived from fiddly little pieces.... But, if one is an artist, one is mad. And if not, one is an idiot.... Who made the universe? I did. Movement creates number, force creates movement, will creates force. And what creates will? Creates, *quid est?* Form and substance, body and soul, the being, the shadow—who can tell one from the other?... And the devil is such an ass he's taken fright at syllogisms and is off... unless it was he invented algebra, with preachers and prostitutes. The whole thing is the work of a done-in devil snoring over his plate. And then louts finger everything with their filthy paws. They are stupidity cubed!... Ah, everything is a desolation of dullness. I want only delicate things that rock sore heads to sleep and dress their wounds.

...Prayer, faith—but it is all *autosuggestion*—oh, do be quiet a little....

Variety

A B C

A T THE BEGINNING there will be Sleep. Animal locked deep in slumber; warm easy mass mysteriously alone; shut Ark of life bearing toward day my histories and futures—you do not know me, you preserve me, you are my ineffable continuance; your treasure is my secret. Silence, my silence! Absence, my absence, O my closed form, all other thought I abandon, to contemplate you with full heart. You have made yourself an island of time, you are a time that has become detached from that vast Time in which your indefinite duration has the subsistence and eternity of a smoke-ring. No deliberation has more of strangeness or of piety; there is no more intimate marvel. My love toward you is without limit. I lean over you, who are I, and there is no communion between us. You await me without knowing me and I am what you lack that you may desire me. You are without defense. What ill you do me with the noise of your breathing! I am too straitly bound to your suspended sigh. Through this castoff mask you exhale the murmur of stationary existence. I listen to my frailty, and my stupidity stares me in the face. Man lost in your own roads, a stranger in your own mansion, furnished with alien hands that fetter your actions, cumbered with arms and legs that shackle your movements, you do not even know the number of your members and ramble astray in their remoteness. Your very eyes have arranged their own darknesses, reflecting nothing at nothing, and their night sees but their night. Alas, how you yield to your matter, conforming, dear thing of life, to the weight of what you are! Lying in such lassitude, with what simplicity do you offer me my shape of least resistance! But I am hazard, rupture, sign. I am your emanation and your angel. We are nothing without one another and yet between us is pure abyss. My vigor, in you thinly dispersed, in me is the hope of hope. A series of insensible modulations will draw my presence out of your absence; my energy, from your inertia; my will, from your fullness of equilibrium and prostration. I shall burst upon my members as a prodigy, I shall drive impotence out of my lands, I shall occupy my empire to its very toenails, your furthest outliers shall obey me and boldly we shall enter into the kingdom of our eyes. . . . But do not be reborn just yet. O rest still, rest *me*. . . . I am afraid of finding unhappy thoughts again. Let us wait separately until the simple monotonous churning of the machines of life has worn or swallowed every grain of the yet dividing hour. I was, you are, I shall be. . . . What will be is a gentle inference from what was. Therefore my anxious tenderness. . . . And now this Thing stirs, this form changes its form, the lips it seems to offer itself sketch out an act of discourse—a speech declaimed by no one to no one, an appeal, a declaration of love, a begging, a mumble, all isolated in the universe, without connections, with no one and no other. . . . Tentative flashes, clumsy groanings toward self-resurrection. And now! here it is, *my* weariness, the miracle, solid objects; my cares, my projects, and the Day!

B OWLING over the shadows and the bed, tense, relaxed; parting, repelling, the billows of the uncertain sheet, the creature at last gets clear of their soothing chaos. The virtue of being Himself invades him. To be Himself seizes him like a surprise—sometimes happy, sometimes exceedingly not. How many wakings had better have been dreams!... But promptly unity claims the limbs, and from nape to heel an event becomes a man. *Up!* cries all my body, *you must break with the impossible!*...Up! The miracle of rising is achieved. What more simple, what less explicable, than this marvel, Balance? Get up now, walk, catch up with your attempts on space; follow your gaze that has taken flight into the visible; advance, step by countable step, into the sphere of lights and deeds; measure your strength against resisting bodies.... And you, a while I abandon you, Sweetness of un-being! I shall forget sleep till night. Good-bye till evening, mysterious games, monsters, murky scenes, and you, vain loves!... Now I divest myself of incognito. Ah, who can tell me how my self has been ferried, complete, across nonexistence or what vessel has carried me, lifeless, yet with all my life and mind, from one shore to the other of Nothing? How dares one sleep? Such trust in the loyalty of my body, in the still night, such faith in the order and constancy of the universe!... Tonight, Absence, you will return! Once again you will resume your few hours' throne, mysterious frightening impotence, quintessential weakness, unbreakable spell that chains the closed eyes to their images. . . . One cannot turn round, held fast in the soft ore of sleep, to catch him in the act—*the Monkey that shows the slides of Dream.* . . .

C ALM, how calm the hour, how softly tinted the young end of night! Pushing back the shutters, to left, to right, with the quick breast-stroke of a swimmer, I launch into the ecstasies of space. It is pure, it is virgin, sweet, divine. I hail you, grandeur proffered to every act of gaze, beginning of perfect transparency! So vast a space, what an omen for the mind! I would bless you, O everything, if I knew the words. . . . Upon the balcony outlined above the leaves, upon the threshold of the prime hour and of all that is possible, I am sleeping and waking, I am night and day, protractedly I offer my unwearying love, my immeasurable timidity. The soul slakes its thirst at the cold spring of time, sips on shadows, swallows a mouthful of dawn, imagines herself a sleeping woman or an angel of light, falls into a study, is sad, flies in the shape of a bird up to that half-naked summit whose deep night-blue is pierced by a crag, all flesh and gold. Some orange tree breathes from the shade. Very high up a few exquisitely sharp but small stars linger. The moon is that chip of melting ice. Suddenly I am painfully aware that a gray-haired child is seeing old sorrows (half ghosts, half gods) in that celestial object of gleaming wasting matter, frail and cold in insensible dissolution. I look at it as though I were out of my heart. Long ago my youth pined, sensing the ascent of tears, at this same hour and under the same enchantment of the evaporating moon. My youth has seen this same morning, and I and my youth stand side by side.... Divided, how may I pray? How pray when another self is overhearing the prayer?—Therefore one must pray only in an unknown tongue. Render riddle for riddle, riddle to riddle. Lift up the mystery in you toward the mystery in itself. There is in you something equal to what is beyond you.

Waiting

(Sketch for a Poem)

... A ND ABRUPTLY I feel a silence and a spirit in the hairs on the back of my neck. Who is then so close to me that I dare not twist my head and seize him in my hand? I know too well that I should bring into being what is not yet.... I know well that I should seize the living thing you are, and that the transformation of all our life lies in my hand. It is then and not there.... Strangeness!...

You are there, with all the inexpressible consequences of the kiss that hangs over us, which nothing now can prevent.

For what are you waiting? You await the moment when you can wait no longer, and in you you feel the growing burden of a fate. Your lips will thud on my nape like a stone.... *Just one more moment, Mr. Hangman!*...

I watch and listen to the clock's pendulum beating like the heart of a world that is a stranger to our hearts. Its time is no longer ours. For me the future is as the past. Something that has yet to be is all done. The walls of this room hold every modality of duration: what was, what is, what will be, freely interchange within its ring. What unfinished thoughts, what overpowering forebodings, are born and die in my mind!

The book before me has become illegible; and on its lines, where my eye fixes in a desperation of unseeing, my soul awaits the stroke.

I shall turn swiftly to face you, when the signal that is in us both springs from you.

Midday

ODOR of fruits and of hot sauce. A simple pleasure in the air. Through the half-open door the steam of cooking meat, and then in comes a woman all rose and ebony who bears the Dish. Its sovereign aroma takes possession of every soul. Moses' miracle of water is re-enacted in every mouth. Faces shine; voices have a brighter ring. One rubs his hands before his virgin plate. Another's eyes are glued to this smoking goodness on its way. The food, dressed and arranged in such a fashion as best to bring about its own disappearance, circulates, curtseys, and offers itself to body after body. Soon the omnipotent spirits of desirable matter have mounted into the heads of men. Politics and literature sparkle amidst the sounds of mouths and table crystal. Tongues are unsheathed; a liveliness, good will, and malice, in overflowing measure are showered on the table-companions, uniting them, then spending them in words between the gulps and chewings.

The big handsome dog crouching between two of them puts one in mind of a statue of Expectation. He would be an Egyptian god of basalt, were his tail not thwacking the floor. Nothing could be readier than the plain act of this simple beast, the eager swallow of this immobility charged with desire, when someone tenders him the alms of bone or gristle, that men find useless. This muzzle, magnetically attached, through the glowing eyes, to the one desire of his animal being, is an infallible snapping-machine, disposing of all the refuse of the human board.

But now at last our mouths weary of flavors: strawberries, coffee, tobacco, tire them in their turn, and the prostration of repletion reduces us to smiles in smoke.

The Bath

In the spotless gleaming sarcophagus, gentle is the lazy water, warm perfect spouse of the body's form.

The free and weightless nude assumes a position of total rest. All is easy in liquid, the unloosed legs as motile as the buoyant arms. The man lays down his height, flowing into the longness his highness has become. He stretches to dilate his spring to the utmost; he equals his sense of his power to let it go. Delicately he shifts from point to point of support; a finger props and lifts him; and his floating forces, half melted into the massy calm of the water, dream of algae and angels. The weight of the happily inundated flesh is almost as nothing; the heat of his blood is little different from that of the enclosing water and it searches freely into every cranny of his skin. The living body can scarcely distinguish itself from the amorphous body whose substance at once replaces it if it moves. An individual is sinking into the generalized saturation about him; someone feels himself insensibly dissolve. The physical man becomes no more than a happy dream of the vague intellect. The moment admires its soft reflection and sees its own limbs limpid in the water's glass. He who observes and speaks with himself is astonished at the size and symmetry of the frame of which he disposes, and the thinking head amuses itself with a foot, apparently very far away, which magically obeys. It sees a big toe rise from the deep, then flex, or a knee emerge, then plunge again in the transparency, like an ocean island that appears and vanishes at a geological caprice. The will itself and the general freedom of the being in the idle water become one.

There is perhaps in the flat steamy air a perfume whose complex bouquet stirs memories, caressing or coloring the vague desires of the nakedness there. His eyes lose focus or close. From lack of contacts time grows weak. The mind opens its wrists in a dream.

Laura

SINCE DAWN she has been with me, Laura, alone in a private sphere.

Solitude I name this closed system where all things are alive. At this first hour that I bank neither with my days nor with my nights, but under a quite separate account, all that is about me shares my being there. The walls of my room are a circumscription created by my will. The light of the lamp is a sort of consciousness. The unscribbled sheet before me is clear and populous as a sleeplessness. I brood over my illumined hands as though they were the pieces of some game of innumerable gambits. The whole complex of every instant is present to my senses.

*

For Laura to appear, all things must be exactly thus, all must ensure my being ideally alone. Laura demands, as she also inhabits, a silence bristling with expectations, in which at times I become what I am awaiting. She catches the whispering between my daemon and my desire. Her white face is indistinct enough, but not her gaze. What a precision of power !...Wherever my eyes settle, they carry hers with them. And if I close my lids at last, her own are widely raised and asking. The power to question of these eyes transfixes me, and sometimes it happens that I cannot bear their unwavering depth any longer.

Then it is that the too enchanting fragrance of the dress that Laura wore, of the hands and of the hair of the real Laura, the Laura who was flesh, is born again from nothing; it dumbfounds my thinking, mingled or thickened with the bitter perfume of the dead leaves one burns at autumn's end, and I fall heartlong into a magic sadness.

The Unique

A THOUSAND times already I have experienced the Unique....

A thousand times and more than a thousand times, that whose essence is to be unique....

"You always permit it to fail to recognize you!"

There is then, in a man's make-up, some power of obliteration, lacking which a single day would quite exhaust and consume the whole world's charm, and a single thought devour his whole intelligence?

But a thirst for knowing, a joy at feeling the approaching Notion come, at seeing an entire realm of mind little by little lit up, is kindled again and again from the banked-up embers of the soul. Each dawn is the first. The idea's advent makes the man anew.

Yet how comes it about that I refuse and annul my self at this very point where hope is born again, regilding as always the lofty pediments of pure Promise, the endless staircase into Knowing, and those mysterious altars where our offered lives are turned to votive smoke about the feet of the idols of the Intellect, and our loves, our bloods, our times are transformed by spiritual acts and prodigious prayers into works and thoughts?

Have I not learned to expect the unexpected? Is not the sensation of novelty the commonest in my world?

Perhaps it is the law of the mind that it should remain ignorant of the most elementary of its laws. A law that insists that no desire shall have known its like. For a desire is all power; but the recollection of a power is impotence, whereas energy is simply my *presence* brought to its intensest point.

Yet, even as the mind's very instant aspires to the fancied unique and I dream of states of being without parallel, every heartbeat reminds me, every breath recalls: that *the most important thing is that which is the most repeated.*

Greeting the Day

I TAKE one pace upon the terrace. . . .

I enter upon the stage of my own seeing.

My presence knows itself the equal and opposite of all this world of light which would pretend to surround it. Here is the whole confrontation of the earth and sky. The hour attempts to seize me and the place believes it has me trapped. . . .

But the place and its hour are no more to the mind than an accident—an incident—one phantom of many. All this daylight is a phantom of my private night.

In vain the sun assaults me with a gigantic image, of miraculous colors, riddling me all the riddles of the seen. . . . There are all kinds of other profferings within me, that are neither of the earth nor of the sky.

This splendid day with all its richness and clarity, bounded by tiles and palms, with all its blue whose achieved plenitude confirms in the zenith its own august form, is no more to me than an ephemeral bubble half filled with objects without point.

Beautiful *Today* that you are—*Today* that surrounds me—I am *Yesterday* and *Tomorrow*. . . . You are only what is, and I am never: I am only what may be. . . . Here, all that shines and pulses is not I.

I take another pace upon the terrace. . . .

I advance, like a stranger, into the light. . . . Who is more a stranger than he who notes himself seeing what he sees?

The pure and burning ground transfixes me with the brilliance of its stretched-out nakedness. Urns, bellies of shadow, are foci of leaves and fires. Dryly the olive brushes off the pinpoint sparkles pestering it. On a roof of rose and primrose sleep four doves: vaguely I sense their bodies' feelings in the soft hot feathers on the warm baked clay, O Life. . . .

What is this country to me? What is this world to me? But also what are the comings and goings in my mind to me, all that is born there and dies?

What I see, what I think—they vie for *what I am.* They know nothing of it; they push it about; they treat it like a thing. . . . *Am I* the object of an idea, or the plaything of the splendor of a day?

The Return

LET US turn back. . . . The gold dies, all softly turns and goes down. The ground smokes. Already a diamond has scratched a prick-hole in the height. The dwellings and domes of leaves grow many and confused; and all the inequalities of earth insensibly assimilate into one vast flock of shadowy forms stunned with sleep. About us, soon, the profound oneness of darkness will be.

The purest essence of existence detaches from us and rises on high. Slowly the pole of stars declares that it is the Whole. Some godhead steps aside from time, while the weight upon it of a done day of our life makes us bow the head. Silence takes us: it divides us, and it joins. Lassitude is all.

There walk with us the mournful shadows of our thoughts (our simplest, grandest, bitterest, emptiest, or most ignorant thoughts). Under cover of dusk the myths emerge, more sensitive and more notable than everything else that is.

Let us turn back. . . . Let us hurry to the flames and lamps! Sit down beside me. You stretch your cold hands and wet feet to the glow, and your eyes are shot with sparks. Life and death leap and crackle before you.

And now you think only of things that are impossible to say; and the outcome of these moments is not to be expressed in words.

All here is sweetness, warmth, wisdom, and security. All the same I am well aware that you sense and accept within you the presence of all the enemies of life. *What will not be, what will be*, those are the opposing powers. And that is why you shiver before the capering flame, and you are feeble and constrained, reduced to the compass of your own locked heart, mute and pitiable in the seeming lap of happiness.

I know beyond a doubt that all the terrors of man, and the terrors of little children, and the terrors of the beasts even are in you because of the hour. There is age, the frailty of the frame, the outer shadows drawing in, the tales and the wolves, the assassins and the ghosts.... One's being is not much protection against the multitude of dangers that steal forth from it, once the night is come. I feel it as though I were in your skin. That is why we must take one another in our arms and, shutting the eyelids tight, embrace a living thing, and hide in another's existence.

Psalm I

I am mounted as by a rider,
Faceless, who drives me against what I do:
He beats me and reins me in, he whips me
With circumstance, breaking me on barriers,
Changes his name, reins me in till I snap.
He mocks my strength
He imposes disorder
He spends my breath
He crunches my heart in his hand.
I cannot catch up with his will;
Like a madman he rides me
And I tremble and gallop
And I cannot turn to see him. I cannot quite see him.
He slips my intelligence.
O ride some other man!...

You Forget

You forget, but your body stays.
You feel nothing, but your body has changed.
You speak, but your body will act.
You see, and it does not.
You walk, and it stamps its feet.
You taste, and it digests,
You smile, it wrinkles;
You sleep, and it sleeps.

It did not know that you were changing your mind.
You did not know that it was changing its might, down
  there in the depths.

Psalm II

A clear idea has undone me,
A truth has led me astray....

What does writing matter?—I was thinking.
Shall I void myself into the word?
It is fickle, and becomes a stranger.
Is it the paper that is to be advanced to perfection?
Or is it I....
And the best of me spent into writing, what have I left
  but my folly?
What comes to me, but is beyond the powers of
  writing, shall I
Reject it?
The most delicate, the most deep, the most particular—
Do we not call them *inexpressible*?

The most faithful, the most quick, the most true, the
  moment—
Are they not dumb?
All books seem to me *false*—I have an ear that hears the
  voice of the author,
Distinct from that of the book.
Never do they speak together.

Two Poems

I

Led by the image I wish you to have of me;
Or to comfort myself, when I am again alone,
By the notion of having defeated you,
Outstripped you into yourself, foreseen your recesses,
Setting a part of my strength against all yours,
Against your utmost....

II

O my strange selves—why are you not verse?
You O Present... and you Forms, Meanings, Functions,
    Phases, Plots:
You, sharpness of clarity, the point; and you the side,
    the without form!
This making new and again, why does it not sing?
But to know one's own thought, how much practice!
In freedom to think that thought, those distinct mo-
    ments, illuminations; to think them as they are.
And, after the courting of the pure ingredients, to wed
    them, be them.
That they at last may live... and relive....

Idea for a Story

(In the style of Villiers de l'Isle-Adam)

AN ENGLISHMAN (or Dutchman) in his fifties, ruddy and blue-eyed, worthy, solid, forthright, etc. One evening, a little drunk, he allows himself to speak of love, and ends by extracting from his wallet something that looks like part of the sole of a shoe, black—revolting—on which have been tooled some gold initials. And he tells the tale of someone who loved him so much that she finally shot at him. Flesh-wound. "She was hanged, gentlemen, that jealous creature was hanged. Irreplaceable. And this? This, sir, is her *tongue*. A pretty penny it cost me. Her tongue, sir, *her tongue*, her TONGUE!"

Short Story

HERCULES was seeing a lot of the Amazons.

What with killing, pillaging, raping them—at random more or less, as though his tremendous brute strength took all these activities casually in its stride.

But one Amazon was prepared. She seemed quite fearless of him. To her clear, absent gaze he appeared not so much a monster as an imbecile. Wrongly, perhaps.

So she stretched out full length and started writing a book.

And this, reclining on the skin of a white bear which she hadn't even killed herself.

"—And what do you do?" Hercules inquired.

"Me?" She wrote down a *pensée*. "I think," she said.

"You *think*?" he echoed. "Then I scram."

Work

I LOVE you, my Work, when you are truly mine. You, whom I recognize through all your changings. You alone, indeed, are truly I, when I master the living system of my nerves or of my thinking forces, when I feel myself enter by swiftest paths into my own durations.

I possess me if you possess me, I am the master if I am your slave and tool.

As the body of the rider mounted by his idea mounts his horse and is one with it.

As the boat between sail and tiller, with the wind, against the wind.

Oh do not let yourself be carried away (as so many have boasted of being) by the only power that is not yours!

Regarding the Sea

S K Y A N D S E A inseparably engage the widest and deepest contemplation: they are the most elemental and elementary things, the freest in appearance, the most changeable throughout the whole gamut of their immense unity; and yet the most constantly themselves, the most visibly constrained to the same states of torment or of calm, of perturbation or of limpid clarity.

Idle, at the edge of the waves, if we try to decipher what is born in us before their presence; when, with salt upon the lips, and the ear soothed or assaulted by the murmurs or by the slammings of the sea, we seek to respond to that all-powerful immanence, we can produce no more than thumbnail thoughts, chips of poems, phantoms of actions, of hopes, of threats—a mere disorder of overexcited whims and overstimulated images aroused by this giantess who offers herself and denies, who invites one's liberties with her seductive surface and repels them with her depths.

That is why no inanimate thing has been more abundantly and naturally *personified* than the sea. One calls it good, bad, treacherous, capricious, mournful, mad, or furious or merciful; one endows it with the contradictions, the changes of mood, the dreams, of a living creature. It is hardly possible to avoid feeling naïvely, when the air, the earth, the moon, the sun, all bring their concurrent forces to bear upon her, that this great fluid body is alive. The wildly arbitrary and self-willed character that the ancients attributed to their gods, as we do sometimes to our women, is inescapably suggested too to dwellers by the sea. A whole tempest is brewed in a couple of hours. A fog bank forms or vanishes as if by magic.

*

Two other notions, too simple in their nakedness, are also begotten by the wave upon the mind.

The first is of *running away*: *to run for running's sake*, idea engendered by a strange sort of *attraction of the horizon*, a virtual launching into the far, a mad desire, blind instinct to depart. The bitter tang of the ocean, the salty breeze that makes us feel we are breathing the bay, the multicolored and multifarious ferment of ports—they marvelously disquiet. The poets of our day, from Keats to Mallarmé, from Baudelaire to Rimbaud, abound in restless lines that ruffle and unsettle us, like sea wind in the riggings of vessels that ride at anchor.

The second notion is perhaps the dark underlying reason for the first. One wishes to escape only what will begin again. The interminable iteration, dumb obstinacy of repetition, the unvarying impact and withdrawal of the rollers of the ground swell everlastingly knocking upon the brink, weary the mind with foreseeing their inevitable rhythm, and inspire in us the absurd notion of an *Eternal Return*. But in the world of ideas absurdity is no inhibition: the insupportably overbearing sense of eternal recurrence transforms itself into a furious urge to break the everlasting cycle, a raging thirst for *unknown foam*, for a virgin time, and events endlessly varying....

*

The sea presents unfailing images of the *possible*—this, for me, is what sums up all its enchantment. How many hours have I not consumed in seeing it without seeing it, in watching it without an inner word! Sometimes its images are all of universals, every wave a life. Sometimes I see no more than the eye does, pictures without names. How to detach oneself from one's vision? How not to fall for the illusions of the lively momentums of the deep, that juggles with transparencies and reflections, with repose and movement, with the tumultuous and the still; that lays out liquid diagrams of law and chance, of chaos and ordained succession; that bars its gates and opens them?

*

The confusions and clarities of a daydream half learned, half childish, accrete about the sea recollections and intellectual flotsam of every kind and age—boyhood reading, memories from voyages, elements of the art of navigation, fragments of exact sciences. . . .

We know now and then that this huge ocean acts as a rein upon the globe, slowing its spinning. To the geologist it is a deposit of liquid mineral holding in suspension atoms of every substance on the earth. Sometimes the fancy will venture into its deeps, enduring their increasing pressure, imagining them growing ever more compressed and dark. It discovers currents in them that are purer, or warmer, or colder, internal rivers flowing in endless ring, splitting, splicing, eroding continents, bearing the warm to the cold, bearing the cold to the warm, melting the icy keels that snap off from the polar floes; forever working interchanges, just as life does, within the fullness of the continuum of the passive mass.

Moreover all that weighty calm is jarred from time to time by sudden shocks, swifter than sound, born of abrupt suboceanic shiftings of its bed. The blind wave hurls itself across a whole divide, fetching up head on against the prodigious foundations of lands and islands, shattering our underpinnings, bringing down buildings, civilizations, lives, and life.

*

Show me the man whose mind has never voyaged in the abyss! As there are certain famous sights that every traveler must see, so there are places and spaces of the imagination, found in every head, artlessly answering to the same irresistible curiosity in each.

We are all poets (as all children are poets) when we think of the depths of the sea, and we stray in them with delight. At every fancied step we raise up dramas and thrills. Inferno for children, whose Virgil is Jules Verne.

Plains rolling or flat, forests, volcanoes, barren canyons, coral churches that wave half-living arms, phosphoric hordes, bushes of feelers, creatures in spirals, clouds of scales —all these imaginable but impenetrable landscapes are much haunted by the mind. We flap in our goggle helmets through colored shadows thrown by liquid skies where sometimes, bad angels of that heaven, fly the prompt heavy forms of cruising sharks.

Upon a rock or in the slime, onto a bed of cockles or of weeds, sometimes comes gently, delicately poising, settling, at the end of a languorous descent, the huge conch of a ship *that has been drinking*. There, two thousand meters down, a *Titanic* encloses an exhaustive collection of the material culture of our day: the machinery, the jewelry, the fashions of such and such a year. . . .

*

But the ocean has also marvels that are real, that can be seen, and yet pass all imagining. I mean such things as submarine forests: what about a wood *floating free*, without roots, yet denser, more intimately entangled, more pullulating with life than the most virgin jungle on land? Consider that Atlantic region, clipped in a loop of the Gulf Stream, that is named the Sargasso Sea, a gigantic mass of suspended sea-weed, a sort of nebula of cellulose nourished solely by the water itself and by all those bodies that the water holds dis-solved. Quite untethered to its sea-grounds, whose mean *depth* is three miles, this strange raft is the size of Russia in Europe, and fabulously peopled with every variety of crab and fish. Its vastness has been calculated: it must contain some million cubic miles of vegetable matter, in which are incalculable reserves of soda, potash, chlorine, bromine, iodine, and wrack.

This colossal powerhouse of life, this mass of organic matter, has been suggested as an explanation of petroleum deposits. The weed, brought to the surface by a raising of the bed of the sea, would be gradually soaked again and worked upon by rain until it decomposed and reverted into hydrocarbons. . . .

The ocean is mysteriously linked with life. If life was born in it, as so many like to think, one understands why in its place of origin it is found so much more vigorous, more diverse, more abundant, more prolific, than on land. Certain regions of the sea, zones intermediary between the surface and the great depths, are occupied by incredible quantities of beings, as certain unstable roads through the formless waters are traveled by them—sometimes more closely pressed against one another than we are in crowds or at crossroads in our capitals. Nothing better conveys the truly innocent nature of life than a shoal of fish. And, to express my meaning better, I would take *fish* as a true singular—making of these *fishes* one single substance; a substance composed, no doubt, of separately organized individuals, but which behaves as a whole as though it were but one, a one that is subjected to conditions and acted upon by exterior laws that are all very simple.

I wonder whether the value that we put on life, the uniqueness and meaning that we attribute to it, the metaphysical fervor with which we proclaim each individual to be an isolated and unrepeatable event, produced once and for all, do not derive in part from the comparative rarity and the low fecundity of the mammals that we are? One finds in the sea that the unconscionable proliferation of its swarming beasts is happily balanced by the mutual destruction they wreak upon one another. There is a hierarchy of devouring; a statistical equilibrium is ceaselessly maintained between the species of *those that eat* and *those that are eaten*.

So death is seen to be an indispensable requisite of life, rather than a repeated but ever newly horrible astonishment. It is on the side of life, not against it. Life must call upon death *in order to live*, each day *breathing in* such and such a number of creatures and *breathing out* so many more; and between these totals a more or less constant proportion must be kept. Life does not like survivors.

When we consider the enormous concentration of individuals in those restricted regions where life is most at home, we impute some special property of the watery childbed swathed about the globe, *maintaining undifferentiable beings* in balance with the condition, composition, climate, currents, of the favored zone.

*

The happiest fellow in the world, I should surely find him in a small school of porpoises. One looks down upon them from the bows and they are seeming demi-gods. Sometimes, all garlanded with foam, they graze the world of air, playing with the fire of the bare sun; sometimes they are at the very stem of the prow, vying with it as it cleaves and parts the burden of the waters, worrying the course, snapping at the ship's nose, like dogs before a horse. Always they embody the double notion of the whimsical and strong. They are powerful, they are quick, they have little to fear; they speed superbly through every dimension of their element, free of weight, regardless of rigid support. They are creatures therefore of a condition we know only in dreams, and that, awake, we seek to re-enter by the back gate of drugs or the *force-majeure* of machines. Free mobility seems to man a supreme state of "bliss": he pursues it with all diligence, he simulates it in music and in dance, he confers it upon the glorious bodies of the elect. These leaping plunging porpoises show him the thing itself, and he fills his heart with envy. This is why he also bestows upon ships, even the ugliest, even the most unwieldy, a gaze impassioned by his universal yearning toward everything that helps him move.

There is no delectable corner—of Alp or forest, site of temples or enchanted garden—that equals, for me, the view from a well-placed terrace above a port. The eye possesses the sea, the town, the contrast between them, and all that is admitted, emitted, confined, at every hour of the day, within the snapped ring of the moles and jetties. I breathe in steam, smoke, gusts, and odors, with the highest pleasure. I love even the hanging dust of straw and coal about the quays; even the outlandish stinks of docks and warehouses,

impregnated with the essences of kerosene, cattle, fruits, of
untanned skins, of sulphur, planks of pine, and coffee. I could
let slip whole days in watching what Joseph Vernet called
"the various works of a sea-port." From the far horizon to
the clean-cut edges of the artificial shore, from the pale thin
mountains of the distant coast to the gleaming whitenesses
of lighthouse and control tower, the gaze enfolds the human
and the inhuman at a sweep. For is not this the exact frontier
at which the eternally wild, brute physical nature, the un-
failing primitive, the ever-virgin reality, meet face to face
the works of the hands of man—the earth arranged, sym-
metries ordained, solids drawn up in ranks, energies directed
and opposed, and the whole apparatus of an effort whose
evident principle is finality, economy, the appropriate, fore-
sight, hope?

Happy these idlers elbow-propped on the parapets of pure
white stone from which the Port Authority constructs its
breakwaters and sea-walls! Others lie prone on the foremost
blocks that the waves endlessly gnaw, mine, and crumble
apart. Yet others fish; or spike their fingers on the motile
spines of urchins, or with a knife prise off the scallops from
the rocks. Ports always boast this fauna of lazy ones, half
philosophers, half mussels. No better companions for a poet.
They are the real fans of the Ocean Theater; nothing of port
life passes them by. For them, as for me, an arrival, a depar-
ture, are ever new and fresh. We discuss small silhouettes
scried across the bay. Some singularity of outline or of
rigging starts us guessing. We infer the characters of captains
from the manner in which they receive the pilots who come
alongside. . . . But I have stopped listening; my eyes distract
me from my ears. A big ship is approaching; the sail of a

smack bellies out and steals to sea. The puffing giant passes the winged dwarf in the mouth, utters a strange bellow and heaves to; out of its hawse-hole pours a stream of links with all the thunderings, screechings, and silvery chinkings of a bucket-chain pulled violently out of its well. Sometimes, just as the rich rub shoulders with the poor in the street, a spotless clean-lined Yacht, all luxury and shine, glides in beside the grubby, dateless barges, coasters, and lighters, laden with bricks or barrels, with ailing engines, with sails all patches, ablaze with rust; whose paintwork is a calamity; whose passengers, some chickens and an unnamable dog. And yet from time to time it happens that the old hulk ferrying these outcasts has still beautiful lines. Almost all the true beauties of a ship are below water: the rest is mere *dead works*. See them on the slips or in the graving-dock, consider the grace and force of the keels, their solid geometry, the most delicate and minutely calculated modulations of their surfaces, which have to obey so many different conditions at once. It is after this that art begins: no architecture can be more subtle than that which erects upon the movable a building which is the mover and the moved.

How to Make a Port

A LANGUAGE glutted with baroque vocabulary, copious, of all epochs, loaded like the Latin of Apuleius, might celebrate (not describe—a dreary chore) all the things that assault the eyes, ears, and nostrils, excite or amuse the mind, in the wharves, approaches, and sluggish waters of a port.

EXCESS AND ABUSE OF WORDS must express the gallimaufry of moments and elements, the confusions of things and people, the multiplicities of devices, manipulations, and events, the tangles of tackle, the spider systems of ropes and wires, the alacrities of launches between the monumental immobilities of the vast opaque bodies of vessels at anchor, the visions of slumbering forces in the agglutinations of the heaped links of coiled chains and in the gross knots and splicings of hawsers and cables, and the bizarre feats of cast-iron Titans and Herculeses that raise their burdens, pirouette, then dump them in deep holds or in the wells of over-cargoed lighters.

THEN BY NO MEANS, DEAR WRITER, omit to belly forth, from gigantic chimneys, mighty whirlpools of darkness, set off from time to time by chance escapes of steam marvelously white; and sing the inconstant flux of omnipresent breeze, made manifest here and there to the eye by the colored pulsing of fluttered ensigns or the burlesque up- heaval of a whole crew's washing-line, with empty legs that skip in vain from the lashings of sharp air, with shirt-arms turned to wings by desperation. . . .

NEXT: create the illusion of that complex sound resulting from all these causes. Draw inspiration from that perfect discord that is the sum of the groan of wood, the clank of metal, the brutally undulating ululation of the winch, the fearful cavernous mooing of sirens, the exacerbated whine of overheated pulleys, the voice of the man with the hoist, the voice of the man with the loud-hailer, the bark of the ship's dog and the outraged cackling of hens, while cattle low awaiting shipment and one of them dances on air, snatched at a swoop to heaven by the crane and girth-band.

NOW ADD quite another harlequinade of sensations, and by no means the least imperious, that mingle as they best may with the visible things on this arena, invading them, be- setting them, exalting them to the most real and inward presence—I mean the intrusions, fluctuations, and diversions of emanations, exhalations, odors, scents, stinks, and aromas, incontrovertible souls of petroleum, copra, coal, hot oil, oranges, and the grease of fleeces, of lees, of drying codfish, of steaming bouillabaisse, of all that by infinitesimal losses of subtle matter sheds into the air avowals of its identity.

BUT SUDDENLY, irresistible brine-intoxicated Archangel, huge hastening spirit of the sea, enter the offshore Wind that in its passing sweeps clear and utterly negates, bears off or disperses, all this abundance of powerful insubstantialities, sharp perfumes, whiffs and stenches, rich disgusting miscellany of the effluvia that are released by life. . . .

Power of Perfumes

PERFUMES amid smells, musical notes amid noises, they stand out clear. They are among the noble, indeed the ideal, elements of our sensation: they inform us of nothing useful, but lay direct hands on our spirits and lead them where they would be forever.

A perfume instantly engenders the desire to breathe it again, and by that is it *Perfume*. It incites a kind of insatiable thirst to gulp in through the nostrils, into the very depths of our beings, the flux of pleasure that it creates. It dilates us: it expands, it makes wildly beat those inward wings of our lungs. The whole machine of our breathing becomes wonderfully intoxicated. Perhaps each of our senses, perhaps each of our organs, has its own tipsiness *in posse*? The eye dazzles with tints, the ear with timbres; but this too gliding odor outdoes all other sensual strength—it topples notions with a voluptuous giddiness to which all will and wisdom yields. It is of all things the most subversive of mental discipline, this incorporeal power that weds with space itself, breeding upon it all the most tenderly fanciful beguilements, the most ready to seduce our virtuous resolutions. The great St. Bernard knew it, when he wrote *Odoratus impedit cogitationem*; his contemplation succumbed to a perfume. How should one follow an argument, or conduct it, or steadily pursue the abstract footprints of the divine essence, if the very air of one's solitude insinuates between each heartbeat the hints and first-fruits of most delicate temptations? How subtle a substance, to alter the whole atmosphere into a spring-head of dreams, a heady craving of lilac or roses, mingling some youthful freshness with giddying and lubricious fumes, slipped in by the cunningest entry! Not that there are not other scents, holy and splendid, released by the spending of rich gums, whose velvet exhalations roll and unroll in the empty hollows of domes and apses, creating ineffable deeps of concentration and waiting before the secret and regal magnificence of the abiding-place of an unknown.

There are good reasons for this singular empire of perfumes over our frames. The other senses are not directly linked to the ordering of our organic life, but that of smell is integrally one with the essential function that, evey four or five seconds, provides us with the means of continuance. One cannot omit to breathe. We float in air: if spicy, the breathed perfume magically makes pleasurable the primary vital act— we must enjoy, to survive. Each time our spirit calls upon its airy medium, it feels this delicious invasion into its most inner room; and more, this intimate sweetness recedes only to exact, with all the force of our will to survive, that it shall in a moment again be what it was. It fades only into the desire from which it is reborn. So perfume alone procures us this sensation as of impulsion into the infinite, arousing, wedding, endlessly rewarding, the advancement of our living forces into time to come.

But we know very little of smell, and the secrets of its mechanics have so far eluded science. Indeed all modes of sensation remain obscure: but in the case of sounds and colors we have at least got to the bottom of the physical agents that give rise to them, we understand their nature and their laws. Taste is a question of chemistry, for both are concerned with substances in a state of change, of dissolution. But how can the smell-bearing particles act? How do these casually peripatetic molecules produce effects so diverse, subtle, or powerful according to their kind? Apart from their actual odor, breathed effluvia provoke side reactions, instantaneously modifying the composition of the blood, acting upon assorted appetites... but for each of us in a different way. Scents hold great sway over our memories, over our feelings therefore. They get into the deepest interstices of our private histories just where they are the most tender and secret. One breath in our nostrils re-creates about us with an invincible illusion of presence a place, a person, a look we were given, and the whole totality of a time lived rears up out of the nothingness of oblivion with all the implacable authority of an emotion that the long years of forgetting have done nothing to pare away. The half-open drawer through whose mouth some linen exhales a fatal aroma lets loose a deadlier thing than ghost or shadow, a real and present power of the past. It is the still living element of an actuality otherwise gone that seizes the existing instant, to master it, for, *of the vanished years, the sole one thing that we can recapture unchanged is perfume, sweet, heady, or smooth.* We breathe now the identical ambergris, the identical jasmine, that we breathed so long ago; and it is this that brings us near to fainting. There is no portrait, handwriting, token, material witness of a tenderness we had thought quite dead, that strikes us with that almost insupportable energy of resurrection of a scent, the sharpest, most forcible poison of the heart.

Paris Is Here

I DREAMED I was at sea.... PARIS awakes me. With complex hum she welcomes me home. She borders and embroiders my silence with all that is taking place outside my walls; alone, she peoples me.

I listen, and my ears and mind strain to pick out and decipher this jumbled medley of unknown incidents and invisible doings, both present and absent from me.

Upon a grumbling rivery ground forever fed by the rolling of the innumerable wheel, a kind of vista of noises, whose aural scenery composes and decomposes every instant, conveys the impression of some gigantic operation accompanied by a multitude of events, independent yet continually making themselves felt, be it one or another.

I plumb this vista at every depth, discerning here the bark of a dog, and here the squawk of a horn; and there the screaming of hammered iron, the bitter howl of cable on pulley, or stone complaining of the rasp, the fearful groan of the grab as it bites its sand-load out of the soil, the forlorn whistling of a train in faraway distress; a distinct voice; or vociferations worn smooth and indistinct.

Across the foreground drags a beggar's lengthily pitiful cry.

All that impact or friction can create in the way of sound calls up before me from all quarters this confusion of names and images, risen upon the horizon of my memory and attention. I hear the mooing, belling, thumping, whining, of the concourse of mechanical forces that shift and maltreat the matter of PARIS.

Hidden PARIS, PARIS the motor in the expanse, the protean cause and mighty creature made of stones and life, which all this inexhaustible flow of dull murmur, exploding to hubbub sometimes, implies—PARIS offers her presence to my thought.

Whence is born in me this daunting and absurd desire: *How to think* PARIS.

How can I dream of mastering, reducing to manageable form, such a monster of hugeness, interconnections, dissembled differences? PARIS, the increment of a site, the work of twenty centuries; PARIS, product of the hands, goods, and economy of a great nation; arena of delight and of pain; sworn target of so many conquerors, some mighty in their names, some in their arms; PARIS, treasury; PARIS, a battle; PARIS, gaming-table from which all the faces of fortune, all the lucky numbers of destiny, glitter into every eye; and PARIS, opus and phenomenon, theater of deeds that echo everywhere, itself a deed of highest rank, offspring in part of statistics, in part of wayward will: but before all things PARIS, a moral entity of the first rank, illustrious heir to the most princely titles, possessor not merely of at once the proudest and the darkest memories, but of the awareness of an unrelaxing mission of the spirit.

To think Paris? ... I am lost at once in the alleys of this attempt. Whatever notion comes, once scrutinized, divides. Scarcely is it sketchily there upon the logical plane of my striving than it is lost amongst a thousand others that branch off from it in prolongations, each a potential father of a hundred books. So innumerable are the concrete beauties and the abstract quiddities of the Great Metropolis that I am as much at the mercy of diverse fancies, in their every possible combination, as is a stranger wandering baffled in the network of our streets, dazed and deafened by the traffic and the din. And now this very image itself seizes the throne, grows great in me, inspiring me suddenly with a strange comparison. I fancy that to think PARIS may be compared, or may be confounded, with *thinking the mind*. I picture to myself the street map of the gigantic city, and nothing could serve as better model for the domain of our ideas, the mysterious area of the swooping hazards of thought, than this labyrinth of paths, some spiderly fortuitous, others rectilinear and direct. . . .

And I ponder that in us too are avenues, crossroads, blind alleys; sinister corners are to be found there, and points one approaches at peril. Charming ones also, and ones that are holy. And the soul has its sepulchers—just as it boasts the monuments to our victories and the tall palaces of our pride. And we know that in our own inward City, whose every instant is a fresh step of our life, an endless activity begets good and evil, false and true, beautiful and horrible, all the contraries that are man's and make him man—just as these are necessarily arraigned into the same violent contrasts by the like living force of the capital.

To *think* PARIS? But how are we to think PARIS, when our minds cannot even embrace the system of a simple organism by properly conceiving the unity that subsists between its functions and its substance, and by understanding what of its environment it imbibes and what it rejects, repels; nor by forming a picture of how it builds itself and grows, of how it establishes its network of interior communications, of how it transforms its surroundings, constituting itself little by little an individual, a being not to be equaled with others, distinguished from all its apparent similars by a history, a set of responses, of sympathies and antipathies, that are its own alone?

Unceasing hum forever in my ears, forever pouring about me the endlessly welling river of the presence of the Town, this mighty murmur rich in eddies that I turn to and consult between two thoughts, as to a slurred voice betokening the real, is the child of enormous numbers. The NUMBER of PARIS invades, besieges, obsesses my mind.

What interrelations, consequences, correlations, combinations; what ends and what beginnings dazzle thought so soon as thought sets herself to consider the mere quantity of mortals co-existent here, acting and reacting, the one upon the other, in every imaginable and unimaginable way, in endless conflict of their every conceivable inequality!... Thought pictures, in this enclave of a few square miles, a furnace of life that is burning into life, a prodigious consumption of beings and doings, a fermenting of plans, an incessant intensity of interchange of signs and actions, of wishes and feelings, whose values and results, crises and outbursts, now answer one another, now reinforce, now cancel one another out, hour by hour of the day. A thousand knots at every instant are being tied or loosed. Many mysteries go underground; and one imagines destiny as fearfully overworked, here where no deep is ever empty, here where hive is stacked upon populous hive.

A dreamy physicist might amuse himself perhaps, in one of his dreams, by attempting to calculate the internal energy of the town. . . . After all, the concentration of several millions of free beings upon a restricted terrain might afford matter for various excursions into analogy. . . . No doubt this crazy problem collapses so soon as proposed; it reduces to the absurd. But its mere formulation serves to sketch out some sort of phantasmagorical notion as to the sheer quantity of life produced and dissipated and consumed within the mass of PARIS. The mere idea of summing the number of paces taken in PARIS in one day, or the number of syllables spoken there, or all the news arriving, silences thought. I think likewise of all the temptations, resolutions, illuminations, and stupidities taking place in minds; of all the daily births and deaths of fortunes, loves, and reputations—which answer, in the intellectual and social spheres, to the shifts of population recorded by the civil registrar. . . . These are fantastic observations founded upon a base of reality, allowing us to conceive of this vast city as a nebula of events, situated at the extreme limits attainable by our mental apparatus.

Earth, of course, can show other comparable agglomerations, some of them indeed still larger. Yet PARIS is to be distinguished clearly from her fellow million-headed monsters, the NEW YORKS, LONDONS, PEKINGS. . . . In fact no city among our BABYLONS is more personal than she, or mistress of so many and diverse functions. For in none of them has every kind of élite of a nation been so jealously concentrated, for so many centuries, so that by her judgment alone each value takes its place in the scale of values, submitting to her comparisons, facing her criticism, envy, rivalry, mockery, and disdain. In no other city has the unity of a nation been meticulously prepared and consummated by so notable and varied a set of circumstances and the ingathering of men so remote in genius and means. In truth, it is in this foundry that our people, the most composite in Europe, has been melted and remelted in the flames of the most lively and warring minds, as if in the heat generated by their acts of combination.

That is why PARIS is something else besides a political capital and center of industry, a major port and universal market, an artificial paradise, a sanctuary of the arts. Her true singularity lies in this, that all these characteristics combine and do not remain strangers to each other. Eminent specialists in every kind of field always end in meeting one another here and exchanging wealth for wealth. This invaluable traffic could scarcely subsist except where, for centuries, every kind of élite of a great nation has been jealously called together and fenced in. To this concentration camp is destined every Frenchman of distinction. PARIS beckons him, draws him, demands him, and, sometimes, consumes him.

PARIS answers to the essential complexity of the French. It was very necessary that provinces, populations, customs, speeches, so unlike should find themselves an organic center of relation, an agent and a monument of their common understanding. And this, in truth, is the great, proper, and glorious function of PARIS.

For she is the head of France, in which are sited the country's organs of perception and most sensitive reactions. Her beauty and light give France a countenance on which at moments the whole intelligence of the land may be seen visibly to burn. When strong feelings seize our people, it is to this brow the blood mounts, irradiating it with a mighty flush of pride.

To think PARIS?...

The more one tries, the more one feels that, on the contrary, it is by PARIS that one is thought.

1937

APPENDIX
From the Notebooks

Forest

1915

The solemn silence of a solitary forest.

The unique noise of a leaf. All those red leaves weighing on a ground nowhere visible.

Trunks of so pure a blue. All those boles at every distance, each closing off its slice of depth, but at irregular intervals, the interstices giving the impression of a transparency, of looking through some restless fluid—beneath the altitude of tall trees you are at the bottom of a sea—the least movement alters, troubles the vision, shifts it to another plane.

Vegetal silence. Of itself a tree makes no sound. All its proper movement is to grow. It allows its fruits to fall. Its dead arms fall as the wind strikes.

A mantle of silence, horror, fright about your shoulders. Something is looking straight into your marrow, spying through the leaves, watching from behind those trunks, all of life is listening, some presence enveloping the forest has found out, and its eye pierces through to where you are.

Beasts, bandits, gods, God—everything is expecting you, watching, menacing. There, even the most beautiful apparition would stir a strange fear. All is suspense, nothing is more than glimpsed. Cold lights and shadows are distributed by the sheer accident of seeds and acorns fallen here from another epoch. Vast patterns, giants strewn by the handful.

Enormous precise details change into one another at every step. An extremely slender and delicate plant ventures to stand out felicitously and clearly to the eye, casting its design on the vagueness. 5:839

The Angel

Angel

The strangeness of things (the sun, man's face, etc.) It is in this that I am an "Angel," and when this feeling comes over me, *I recognize myself*. And I fall into an ecstasy—but as if I were awaking from habit itself. (To *dream* is also to awake from the comprehensible, from the non-arbitrary—to know the *Actual*, which is nonsense, pure chance, absurdity itself.)

My disbelief is made of this, and of a sense of the possible combinations—of the indecency of a life and specific things; the stupidity of involvement. I look at my face, my characteristics, everything, as a cow looks at a train.   8:880

(Beatrice) "Angel"

Psalm

I am not where you see me. I am not where you think. You love, or hate, a phantom.

My mirage makes you thirsty. My appearance annoys you. My outsides walk and talk. . . . From far away I inhabit the man who is with you.

Because of some sin, an angel was cast out into the body of a man. The memory of his former condition was taken from him. What is any soul that has lost its memory? All that remained of the angel in him was the sense of not being what he was before—the angelic sense of *ubiquity* had not been destroyed in him, being indestructible.

He was subject to the human condition of being *in one place at a time*, but he could not accustom himself to this, and he was always unhappy because he could not, as we can, know one thing at a time, since it was his essential nature to grasp all things in a non-temporal mode, by their principles.

He understood nothing by way of what he was, but everything by way of what he had been and no longer knew:

That was *Me*. This is a portrait.... 15:812

1932

*The Angel**

The angel at last realizes that the law of his tastes is to avoid what is "Human"—Love, Intellect, Poetry (pure!).

Rejection of the forces-in-oneself, denying them.

Rapid exhaustion of... Everything.

Precise memory very weak.

Wide-angle lens—

Transcendence.

External anidolatry and acute inner idology.

Negation: *autotomy* of the acquired.

Mania for secrecy: the theocryptic, the esoteric.

Jealousy of the essence.

Everything that is "human" or ignoble or mean—

* Cf. the prose poem of 1926–27.—J.M.

Pleasures, definite amusements, interests.

But then, what is generally *base* is no more *base* than the rest.

Misapprehension as creativity.

Inefficiency in practice, when practice requires more than *seeing* a solution.

Denial of the serious.

In short, characteristics that would be those of a discrete essence lodged in an *individual*.

Remarkable traits. Fear of working in the fields. Man more destructible than a bird.

Weakness of the instincts. Everything done by mind.

Taking sides with the enemy. The pure Self.

In Love: theological ideas. The *infinite* comes in. But is it even *Love*?

Surprise is essential.

The human: a strange and unnatural fact. Homo is a savage.

The "natural" seems bizarre, arbitrary;

the existent is belittled by its possibilities.

—Things are neither large nor small in the eyes of this Species.

Formula kills repetitions—the everyday.

The individual is a limitation of his mind. Every man is less than his Self.   10:721

1932

"The Angel," Degas called me.

He was more right than he could believe.

Angel = strange = stranger . . . strangely foreign to "what is" and to what he is. I cannot *believe* either in the *sub* or the *ob-jective*: that is, I feel that nothing, not even oneself, could be of interest except in crossing some strange threshold—itself an illusion, and moreover uncrossable....

What am I doing here? is my characteristic reflex question, always nearby.

Faire sans croire—my motto..."do, without believing." I have a horror of believing, and a horror of not doing.

Doing? But "to do" also has its particular meaning for me. It is not: to be engaged in some work. It is: to change *in myself* the one who changes the datum. To disengage oneself, not to be merely the self one was. How many things under *our very eyes are invisible*! Even on the retina, they are still as unperceived as if they did not exist.

"Objects," *expected* things, deaden the sensations....

15:716

Psalms

1938

Psalm

My mind thinks about my mind
My history is different from me
My name fades and my body is an idea
I am what I am
What I was is with all the others
Etcetera.   21:114

1939

Psalm N

Hear, my Lord, what the moment is singing through this
open window filled with plants and trees and the blue and
various depths strewn with roofs like dots—streaked with
flight, populated with murmurs and chirps....

It says that if you were glad to overflowing with all
desirable things, in the plenitude of happiness, unable to
find a flaw in the day, a spot on the sun, a fleck in the
moment, any crack, or spot of rust, etc....

Still, there would always remain the frightful response to
all this perfection ... etc.

The perfect destroys itself. What could be more destructive! The fruit engenders the worm, and the zenith the nadir.

The eternal is the moment that suffices to consume all time.

Etc.—Life, how can you be reborn from death, where your pleasure is?

Etc. You did not love me, then, since you can recover your breath and sight. . . . 22:291

1939

Psalm

And the Eternal said to him:
You shall not write for men!
Beasts they are! Men are beasts,
A worthless race!
I made them of a bit of earth,
At one breath I endowed them
With a show of independence,
And they believed they were worth something. . . .

A bit of breath, a bit of earth
Really costs nothing at all.

But you, since you query me,
Since your eyes are drawn toward the void
And ask of it My opinion:
Listen, listen:
If you believe in writing,
Write for what you would be
And for the beings who would be
IF . . . I were an entirely different god
One you have not yet dreamed of! 22:561–2

1941

Psalm

At the window, suddenly,
A lovely thicket of leaves of several greens
Gently disturbed by the wind, the sun ...
And behind me the latent presence
of vague causes of discontent
like a volume of bitterness in the silence,
bringing resentment against the moment now
   departing,
That sweetness that disturbs,
That flow that mingles the branches and un-mingles
   them
and the coil-spring of their nature brings them back,
and the being of willow is preserved.
At the window, suddenly,
I perceive
A sort of "metaphysical" distance
Between what is seen—and this Me,
A sort of *distance* between my eyes
and me—that
Measures some state of deepening study,
A distance ...
Between what is and what I am ...
And yet, my *looking* is what is. ...
What is that "distance"?
It is perhaps the sensation of withdrawing
not only from some passionate
predilection—but toward the renunciation
of the very *faculty* of producing that
power of preference which is all-powerful: *love.*

... The lovely thicket of leaves divagating
in the wind that divides them, making them speak ...
to the wind, to the heart of ME, to my eyes upon them,
   to my age, my *being*.
      A "being," at the center (always)
of "things" (for it cannot *not* be a center)
a body strangely endowed with the past—
an imminence, an implex, an aside, an oddity, a blank:
my *Self*.   24:691

Crusoe

1898

A prehistoric vision.

A whole population of Crusoes, materialistic to the
extreme. They live in a luxury that today is impossible.
Their tables and the blocks of wood used as furniture are
cut from the deep heart of massive trunks of trees, millenial
hickory or mahogany, of a texture like stone, and on them
shine the richest oils, taken from magnificent animals, the
purest specimens of moving and edible objects. . . .

Flint, the luxury of really pure water.   I:497

1906

Am I not the Crusoe of the mind? Exiled in himself,
reconstructing on the island of his will his own truth: and
the tools it requires. Now to the hunting ! . . . the fishing !
even the parrot is not far away.   4:135

1911

Crusoe.

Startled, seeing a human footprint in the sand; suddenly
enlightened, grown taller, inspired, a mixture of new light

and questions, and full of necessary but incomplete consequences. This is myself waking up, recapturing my night's dream as a dream. What? Wasn't that organized adventure *real*, and didn't I actually *do it*? So that strange parenthetical performance, probable as truth, clever as complexity, and requiring either a mechanism or some man...has no cause? Neither false, since it happened of itself; nor true, since it is outside the order of things—neither false nor true; neither witnessed nor willed.

Who, when, where, and how? What savage visited this shore? Who left this imprint of a man on me? A man asleep is no longer a man, but the substance of a man, something to be created.

And whoever conceived this night's dream was not intelligent.... Isn't it this impersonal faceless thing which, in the act of obeying, teaches?

Feast of fools and slaves. Recompense for the day-long subjection.

On one hand, the dreamer *sees* only the unforeseen.

On the other, he responds only with the well known, the logical, the admissible.

But to *see* what ought to be merely felt, apprehended, glimpsed—that's the strange thing.   4:532

1913

Any man is inferior who is adapted to circumstances that are not present. Crusoe is superior to Friday when things allow for distraction. If things allow less and less distraction and leisure, Friday is superior to Crusoe.

4:899

1915

If there is to be originality, there must be at least three literary Crusoes on the island. *A* imitates *B* who imitates *A*, but *C* imitates neither *A* nor *B*. He takes care *not* to imitate them.   5:679

1922

Crusoe's book
Description has weakened the powers of understanding.
                                                                      8:836

1925

Crusoe
Classical works are perhaps those that can lose their immediate interest without perishing—or turning stale. Is the notion of *preservation*, which is hidden in the idea of perfection and achieved form, the essential idea?—the entirely primitive idea, the Egyptian idea, almost idea as natural law—since life is its act.   11:62

1925

Rimbaud Crusoe
Crusoe *in terra incognita—in ipso*
anima in sensibus.   11:91

1925

Mythology
Man's effort in thinking is to carry over from the shore of shades to the shore of things the snatches of dream that

have some form by which they can be grasped—some resemblance, or use.

When the ship of dreams runs aground on the reefs of waking, Crusoe struggles to bring back something of value to the shore. He labors. 11:96

1926

Simplified types that have come into usage:

Crusoe: man alone, how he makes out.

Hamlet, etc.: man encumbered by moral and religious matters.

Faust: man passing from knowledge to instinct, consciously, and from "learning" to power—even innocent power.

Guignol: man of the people, in cities. 11:459

1926

Crusoe

The tendency to satisfy, successively, every need and desire that makes itself felt.

And it is this successive periodic group which is *true time*, forming the *heavens* and the zodiac of the living man.

Hunger, thirst, fatigue, the desire for movement, the need for excretion, procreation, simple change, these are concerns that appear one after the other. 11:723

1927

Once Crusoe is on his island, the bundles of banknotes mean nothing to him. 12:687

1929

See thought "just as it is."

Philosophers are poor judges of it. The existence of books is deceiving, as the existence of the pyramids is, about man's strength. Accumulation of elements of time . . .

Therefore, at the base: the *moment* and the *man alone*.

Man alone: Crusoe, the man with no "foreign" memories and the Circumstance—   13:417

1931

I am Crusoe. . . .

But the island is even smaller than it seems. There is none smaller. Or rather, it is infinitely small. . . . The Self is infinitely small compared to *anything*, by the very act of becoming distinct from it.

It would require a miracle of notation and expression to "write" the forms of the inner mechanism of a "Self," the language of that total function in which what we call, roughly, simultaneous and successive, external and internal, instantaneous and prolonged, question and answer, received and produced, continuous and discontinuous . . . and the Eternal Present the hub of the function in so far as it is perceptible. . . .   14:890

1931

The notion of Sincerity (Gide's kind) leads to picking one's nose in public and letting go altogether in the presence of others. The existence of others requires that we "repress," consent to hide, consider as non-existent, certain things which, if confessed or practiced without shame, would finally reduce the Self to nothing—as a result of the general ease and absence of constraints. (Cf. thought, interior monologue, the nude.)

(Crusoe, on reflection, re-invents constraints, hides from himself, puts on clothes.)   15:208

1932

In short, simply a mind, with no philosophy or prejudice (in the form of words and verbal responses), reflecting on what it is and what it sees.

This is another Crusoe. Amongst the wreckage of the ship, he finds objects he doesn't know the use of.

Also, the whole of classical culture and the theological tradition are unknown to him.

The impossibility of *belief*, the ingrained habit of verifying...   15:555

1932

Crusoe thinking:

Whoever taught the beaver the art of construction, denied it to many an architect....

Who invented building?—the simple tent, the cave, the tree, the cabin, the earthen wall, the picket fence, the tomb and its role.   15:814

1932

Crusoe thinking:

Man is inconceivable in isolation. Ditto, the bee, the

termite. In defining him, connected plurality is essential. He is one element in the group of men.

Otherwise, language disappears, and with it the additive function of the mind—and man is no longer *man*; he is outside humanity, since humanity requires to be penetrated through and through by the means of communication between like beings, or between anyone and himself—which is thought.

To think is to communicate with oneself. The possibility of a dialogue. The I has no face, no age, no name; and another I has *my* name, *my* face.   16:75

1938

Ego

The difference between individuals depends in part on their training, in part on their sensory-*muscular* and psychological diversity.

For example, with me, muscular inferiority has played a capital role: "I have more nerves than muscles."

Hence: quickness, consciousness, a dominant separatism of imagination, abstentionism, both reserve and reserves, physically lazy but vivacious. In addition, *a weak voice*— I have never yelled. Whence (perhaps) my horror of crowds. Crusoe-ism.   21:134

1938

Ego-Crusoe

I have never been able to learn anything except from myself. I can never understand anything except by *re-inventing it, out of need*. It is only then that the results enlighten and serve me. As if, in me, every root passes through the *center*, or *stops short*. This is difficult to explain and express.

I am terribly *centered*. 21:162

1939

Crusoe

The world of man—what a strange development.

How painful it is to owe everything to someone else! To be born and fed by someone else, to be oneself only through language, which tells me this and yet was formed in me by others, by so many others that they amount to nobody.

If you examine this structure with my eyes, you will see that you don't really know where you begin or where you end—where or in how far you are, positively, neither the physico-animal world nor *Other People*, but actually the unique, the auto-type, the insoluble—and you will feel that you are both strange and indistinguishable from others.

22:794–5

1941

Ego

I was a superlatively mediocre student. It cost me Greek and a good deal of Latin, to say nothing of mathematics! My teachers (except one) taught only by the use of force.

This drove me later on to do as Crusoe did. 24:510

1944

"A Sort of System"

My good old System at times comes to the surface of a

moment. Sometimes one aspect, sometimes another, of that Body of my *thinking and thinkable nature* emerges, poop or prow.

My *thinkable nature*? That which has, on certain occasions, responded as "me," with particularly...satisfying effects of lucidity, constancy, generality.

Such were the notions I created, not as philosophers or scholars do—but according to needs no one had noticed. That is how I discovered that I was a Crusoe of the mind....

28:763

Rachel

1930

Rachel or Emma?—or other names.

In the eighteenth century, the given names of women of the lower classes were quite various and strange.

Two meanings of the word *Life* in literary usage. Goethe seems to me a conjurer. He fabricates a dissolving "depth," a sort of ... superficial "depth"—gilded images.   14:401

1932

"Rachel"

I was soon aware of a remarkable difference between Rachel and Rachel: the one I had imagined in the absence of the other, the other being the one I could see, and actually saw, in person. I called them R and R^1. The first was present when absent; the other, absent (or worse) when present!

But this was to assume that I had an idea of the one present, along with the image of the one absent—and that in the presence of the one present I felt the absence of the one absent!

Such are the effects of overstatement.

In the presence of R lovable and independent, the image of R^1 in bonds. The one [   ] would like her to be.

Rachel

Love, she said, is one of the mind's great occupations, based on a problem of domination. In short, it is a political problem, i.e., how to acquire or hold power over someone.

It's a game. We want, madly, to be able to think of that person with joy and certainty.   15:502

1938

Rachel

An ideal is a limit.
The infinite is stationary.   21:423

1938

Agar . . . ex Rachel

She woke and thought. . . .

Having thought for some time, she broke off this primitive sequence, considering it naïve. She saw that her thoughts were, in fact, a manifestation of *bad feelings*. "I detest them," she said (to some person or other assumed by what she said). "I hate them not as wicked and ugly, but as feelings. . . . But this is itself a feeling ! I shall never get to the end of this. . . ."

21:459

1942

"Rachel" (or Agar).

How can anyone *not* think that existence is *stupid*? That is the problem, Reverend Father. And if we must humiliate ourselves, take on the stupidity that seems the lot of created things, that is to belittle the question itself, and deny that we can be interested in a creator.   26:351

1943

Rachel

"But how can a really living mind, Father, not want to create its own faith? Everything that we learn from others, whether men or books, is nothing but words, and examples. The *value* never comes from anyone but ourselves. Now your job is to force upon us, or snatch from us, that essential gift. Any means will do, to take away our welfare: threats, promises, seduction, logic surprised. You frighten us, you play on our feelings, you reason with us. To convince is to conquer—overcome the resistance of a mind, a character, a sensibility."   27:552

1943

Rachel's Curious Prayer.

"Lord! Grant me the favor that my feelings may despise what my mind despises. Amen.

"But then ... what becomes of You, God!"

"But then," said God, "then, my child, what becomes of your love, and everything that gives value to your life?"

("Philosophical" commentary on the speeches above: "How can there be any disagreement?")   27:714

1944

Rachel

God is everywhere and the Devil on all sides.

There is nowhere to go.   28:23

1945

AMOR. "Love." In this term, there's something like *willing in spite of yourself.*

"Rachel": Elise, or Agar, or Rachel...? sums up the problem of Love, seeing in it one particular aspect of the problem of the OTHER—and formulates it in these questions:

(1) What can be done about an *Other*?

(2) What can be done *with* an *Other*?

"But," answers Rachel (or Agar or Elise), "what does he do about you?" And here we are again, with the problem: the *Other* vs. the *One*. That is, the chemical combination: Like/Unlike (LU UL), to which I was led by an analysis of *Language*, with a view to the analysis of *Law*.

But this kind of research has no end.

Here the theory (UL LU), my fourth act of *Luste*, Rachel's diary, and my own personal feelings are all in contact, or connected, or in opposition = a *Diablerie* of the Mind and of the "heart-sensibility resonance."

It is an incredible thing that there should be *Others*.

29:874

The Island of Xiphos

1943

"Mystery" or on the independence of *Why* and other questions.

The ability to *place*? anywhere.

Why can't I lift a weight of two thousand pounds? This is just as "mysterious" as anything else. Yet no one thinks about it, or bothers about it.

Why then can't I understand how a germ carries so many possibilities (among them, death)? Imagine a germ that cannot carry death!!

But why these *whys*?   27:103

1943

The island of Xiphos is that strange place where the primitive, the archaic, and the future possible come together. A place of non-present contacts. In the forest, the beast called *Intellect*, the dragon of Purity, etc., prowls—*quaerens quid devoret*.   27:145

298

1943

Of the true philosopher. *Phi* at Xiphos.

The knowledge he gets from others and for which he cannot answer in person is often the philosopher's poison. He must beware of literature and secondhand products gotten by means that are not his. He should tell himself that he is an artisan and an artist at transforming ordinary notions into exquisite expressions, and let him seek no other truth than his own.   27:154

1943

(Ego) Xiphos.

The ideal *thought*, for me, is the very contrary of deep;— it is what Leonardo *makes* with these words: *O sun, who never see a shadow!* There is the sublime.

But (taking the attitude of Nietzsche's *Mega*), I say to myself pompously: "Am I not the first, at least among the moderns, to have dared say that philosophy is a matter of form, and to dream of giving shape to 'thoughts' by fashioning combinations similar to those we call 'verse,' by the use of certain *conventions*?" (A line of verse is often built around a nucleus of words by a series of substitutions, *in the presence* of a condition that awaits the satisfying solution.)   27:161

1943

At Xiphos, it was forbidden to teach what no one can know, or to publish anything whatever without proof, when it was a question of things held to be true. This was in the southern part of the island. In the North, it was exactly the contrary and nothing could be stranger than this division of the Island. It might have been said that all the *ones* were in one part and all the *others* in the other, as if someone had operated on a people and separated its mixture of constituent individuals to make of them two *pure* peoples: the fools and the intelligent, the Sympathicotonic and the Vagotonic, the *S* and the *V*. But several other arrangements were tried. In one case, all the *S* women with the *V* men and all the *V* women with the *S* men.   27:174

1943

Xiphos?

Philosophy of?

The great plan to go beyond language

The examination of verbal Idols

The Speaking Head and the thousand and fifteen absolute dice.   27:387

1943

Xiphos: the Temple

There should be a god who would allow himself to *be denied*, who would consider a good demonstration of his non-existence as the free mind's homage, first that such a mind should be concerned with a god, and next would not bother trying to believe something it could not believe.

Although he would be a god, or rather because he would be a true god, he would know that in any man's being there is nothing, there *can* be nothing, which is not reducible to a product of the human mind, and that the *infinite* which figures in the language of men amounts to very little, to the illusion, simply, of a new beginning that takes itself to be an endless extension.

"That's a strange god," I murmured....

"On the contrary," replied Mnéandre, "He is as little strange as it is possible to be. He is the One who considers all other gods as particular cases. They are made of a mental and sentimental substance variously fashioned. But as for Him, He is to those other gods what light is to all forms of matter. 27:583

1943

The preparation of dreams.

Harmonious dreams, corresponding dreams.

Dreams used for creating possibilities.

Education: the students are shown a man whose reflexes are being played upon. He is made to fly into a rage, to have an erection, to fall asleep, etc. What is a man capable of? His implexes, his memory, his strength. 27:633

1943

Xiphos?

What, O sage, is a thing *that doesn't exist*? This attribute delights me. What is a void?—who could paint a beautiful lacuna, a nothing, an absence? We must say that these exist, since here are the names for them, and we are aware of the intervals between things and the silences between sounds.

Perhaps these cavities in the *existent* are the authentic lodgings of the soul. And it is in the most durable and vast of them that, as soon as we are dead, the soul will begin to be no more, endlessly?

But beyond, there is quite certainly such a void that this terrible name fits it only as an empty analogy, since it presupposes a certain presence and a thought, that is to say all the existence one could wish, including non-existence itself, in the form, say, of an idea.

We cannot imagine such an absolute state of non-being, dear Lucien, the god himself would be easier for us to conceive.

Notice that the existent exists only because we are able to think that it does not exist, and that nothing is existent which our thought does not suppress, either by a sort of act or by what is meant by forgetting, or again, because existence is so uninterruptedly and invariably present that, as a result, it is not felt—or again, because it is beyond our powers of apprehension, or this side of them, since our lyre has only five or six strings whose combined sounds furnish only what they can—but, at the same time, they excite us with the idea that many others might be possible, provided there were other means. . . .   27:707

1944

Most people can scarcely bear the Truth. There is a painful sensitivity to the clear and flawless expression of Things.

No one can will all that exists. The great maxim.

*

The sage, ivory-colored and with closed eyes, is to be found under a certain tree on the Island, like a fountain of truth: he tells truth like an automatic instrument. Without thinking, since he is made that way. *Every question* answers itself in him by its own effects (without any reflection at all).

"A brave man is at times useful, often dangerous, always difficult."

"Purity and truth are the most active of acids."

"Terrible are the consequences of the most noble wills, for what is noble is inhuman."   29:187

Acem

The story of Acem or Azem, dictated by him, with no idea beyond these opening words: "There was once a man whose name was Acem or Azem."... And in my head, in the vaguest possible state, a mixture of Teste, the Arabian Nights, recollections of Schwob in his armchair, looking waxy and fat...

The other day, walking about in the rain, feeling agreeably vague, and no less wandering among the fabrications and fantasies of my mind than through the streets... I came back and jotted down this impression of exchanges between Φ and Ψ [Body and Mind]. A formula of no consequence. Today I feel that *I can* add this to the story of Acem (if I should write it), and I conclude that a number of independent circumstances are necessarily brought together in a reader's mind and may increase the sensation of *life*. *Incoherence is what is most real.*   26:563

1943

Acem? My God does not believe in god. He dislikes belief—knows it is a shabby practical necessity.

He has actually taken my sins upon himself.   27:4

Agatha

Perhaps we go beyond the Agatha series ab ab ab etc. because we conceive $(a+b)$ simultaneously.

We cannot imagine a 3-dimensional space any more than a 4-dimensional one. 1:484

The distinction between Φ and Ψ [Body and Mind] is the result of an *attempt* to transform one into the other. (Cf. the general theorem of my method.)

Transformation of *means* into *ends* and *ends* into *means*— ("ends" and "means" taken in the strict, purely subjective sense). 1:644

Ag—I am so entirely present in all the parts of my existence that I cannot conceive of any others. 2:255

1928

(For Ag.[2])

This woman cannot live without astonishing; and knows it; but she is neither stupid (with that exception) nor vulgar —i.e., wishing to astonish only the non-vulgar.

She is capable of work and amazing effort in assembling the means to surprise others—but still with that *honesty* spontaneously produced by the Self (so that it can tolerate its inner self without suffering) and which says to itself at moments of self-awareness, catching itself in the comic act of uttering with authority things it knows it could not justify in depth—"my real weakness is temporary; I mimic my true ideal; I want to be what I appear to be, and I need the stimulus of the appearance I put on, in order to have the strength to pursue and acquire the reality of that appearance."   13:328

NOTES

NOTES

THE TITLE *Poems in the Rough* is a loose-fitting phrase meant to cover a variety of forms—prose poems, free verse, "broken stories," sketches, observations and epigrams, even dreams.

The Appendix to this volume is a series of selections from Valéry's Notebooks, which throw additional light on his conception of the fictional characters and places he had created and developed over many years in his prose poems: Crusoe, Rachel, Acem, the Island of Xiphos, Psalms, the Angel, and Agatha.

The selections and translations in Appendix and Notes are the Editor's.

Introduction, by Octave Nadal

Nadal's essay, written for this collection of Valéry's prose poems, was published in French in a volume of Nadal's essays, *A Mesure Haute* (1957). It has been translated here by Jackson Mathews.

Octave Nadal is former professor of French literature at the Sorbonne and the leading French authority on Valéry. He has written critical studies of a number of major French poets and dramatists from the seventeenth century to the present: Corneille, Molière, Vigny, Nerval, Mallarmé, Rimbaud. Of Valéry's work, he discovered and edited the

Valéry-Fourment correspondence and a number of Valéry's unknown early poems; he has made critical editions of *La Jeune Parque* and *Charmes*, and is now engaged on the biography of Valéry's early years, *La Jeunesse de Valéry*.

xiv. *O dieu démon démiurge ou destin*: Valéry was baptized Ambroise Paul Toussaint Jules, and had thought of using his first name, Ambroise, as the title of this poem written about 1920. Two other versions are entitled "Ambroisie" and "Abeille spirituelle." The present text first appeared in *Les Cahiers du Sud* (Marseille), April, 1957.

xvii. *Paradox on the Architect*: see Collected Works, Vol. 4, pp. 178–87.

xix. *Rue Gay-Lussac*: when Valéry in the mid-nineties began living regularly in Paris, his home for several years was the little Hôtel Henri IV in the Rue Gay-Lussac, just off the Boulevard St-Michel near the Luxembourg Gardens.

xx. *Un creux toujours futur*: literally, "an always future emptiness," from the eighth stanza of *Le Cimetière marin*.

POEMS IN THE ROUGH

3. PARABLES: "Paraboles," with twelve watercolors by L. Albert-Lasard, first published in a limited edition by Maurice Darantière (Epinay-sur-Seine, Les Éditions du Raisin, 1935); see *Œuvres I*, Pléiade (1957), p. 197.

Lou Albert-Lasard, painter and writer, translated a volume of Rilke's poems into French: *Poèmes,... avec une préface de Jean Cassou et un portrait de Rilke par L. Albert-Lasard* (Gallimard, 1937). She later wrote a book on Rilke: *Une Image de Rilke* (Mercure de France, 1953).

The epigraph is translated from Rilke's poem "Die Flamingos," written either in Paris in the autumn of 1907 or on Capri in the spring of 1908. It was first published in the second volume of *Neue Gedichte* (Leipzig, November, 1908). The poem in German has the subtitle "Paris, Jardin des Plantes."

8. IN PRAISE OF WATER: "Louanges de l'eau," appeared first as "Préface" to a brochure of three articles on Perrier mineral water, published by the Source Perrier (Aux Éditions Publicitaires, 1935); see *Œuvres I*, Pléiade (1957), p. 202.

The Perrier Springs are in the region of Montpellier and Sète, the scene of Valéry's boyhood.

12. THE ANAGOGICAL REVELATION: "La Révélation Anagogique," first published in *Histoires Brisées*, Gallimard, 1950. The title is probably modeled on Baudelaire's "Révélation Magnétique," itself a translation of Poe's "Mesmeric Revelation." Poe's influence might also account for Valéry's adding an epigraph *in English*: "An abstract tale"; see *Œuvres II*, Pléiade (1960), p. 466.

The original version of "La Révélation Anagogique" (1938) is found in Valéry's *Cahiers* (21: 70–1). It is longer than the printed text, but not otherwise different. The part found only in the *Cahiers* is translated here (continuation of part 2):

If, however, you examine what you see there, you will observe that the stranger is doing what you feel yourself doing.

So it is the correlative variations that will prove to you that this person is *you*; that he is not capable of *one act* more than *You*.

And for that reason this You is situated somehow in the Anti-Ego and becomes a part of it.

3. In this way, certain characteristics of topology, of limits, of common-quasi-measurement occurred to me and led me to a system of *absolute* notation—which excluded explanation in favor of useable representation and the possibility of translating everything into real abilities.

4. Hence, the will to push the function of the *Self* to the extreme, and not to *personalize* it more and more (which is the phenomenon we notice in waking, in repetitions, etc.)

14. THE ANGEL: "L'Ange." In one of Valéry's notebooks for November–December, 1921 (*Cahiers*, 8: 370) there is an early draft of "The Angel." Twenty-four years later he made the final version. It was his last poem. The text is dated May 1945, two months before his death. It appeared first as a *plaquette*, published by the *N.R.F.*, June 15, 1946; see *Œuvres I*, Pléiade (1957), p. 205.

17. MIXTURE: first published in a limited edition, *Mélange de prose et de poésie, Album plus ou moins illustré d'images sur cuivre de l'auteur* (Les Bibliophiles de l'Automobile-Club de France, 1939); later enlarged and revised, without illustrations, as *Mélange* (Gallimard, 1941); see *Œuvres I*, Pléiade (1957), p. 283. In the Preface to the 1941 edition Valéry said:

This collection consists of a sort of album of highly miscellaneous pieces that I brought together for collectors a while ago, having illustrated it with a dozen or so etchings and added a number of further pieces here included for the first time. No book's title could be more accurate. The disorder that "reigns" (as the phrase has it) in *Mixture* extends even to its chronology. A few items first saw the light nearly fifty years past. Some are almost of yesterday—between the short poem "Disaster" and the "Cantata of Narcissus" nearly half a century has drifted away. This stretch of time is of no importance where intellectual creation is concerned; but, in selecting these two pieces from my papers to bring them together in this volume, I was puzzled to know how they could be recognized as belonging to the same author, or how anyone could decide which was written first. And I confess that these questions would have put me to considerable embarrassment had I not, by definition, been in possession of their answers. This is an old man's problem: he knows very well that he is the *same*, but he would be hard put to it to provide convincing proof of this little proposition. The "I" is perhaps no more than a convenient symbol, as empty as the verb 'to be'—both technical terms, the more convenient for being empty.

25. *No palaver*: the French here is "sans phrases!" The Abbé Siéyès voted for the execution of Louis XVI with the words "La mort sans phrases" ("Death! and no palaver").

26. CHILDHOOD AMONG SWANS: "Enfance aux Cygnes." The translation is by Jackson Mathews. This piece describes an actual incident in Valéry's childhood. See *Œuvres I*, Pléiade (1957), p. 297.

41. *You never invented thunderbolts*: "Tu n'as pas inventé la foudre!"; a pun on the phrase "Il n'a pas inventé la poudre" ("He didn't invent gunpowder"), i.e., he is not very intelligent.

47. *I see at my feet the fragments of the vase*: see p. 127, "Philosophy of the broken vase."

Sully Prud'homme, though he wrote several volumes of verse, is known for one poem: "The Broken Vase" ("Le Vase brisé," *Stances et Poèmes*, 1865). For half a century or more, French schoolchildren had to analyze and memorize this poem—a fact that was of course in Valéry's mind. What is interesting is that he treats the figure of the broken vase seriously, perhaps with the hope of reviving some of the poem's meaning and dignity.

59. POEMS IN THE ROUGH: The title is Hilary Corke's translation of the phrase "Poésie brute," a part-title in Valéry's *Mélange*. There Valéry had brought together, as here, a variety of subjects and forms: prose poems, both free and formal verse, aphorisms and epigrams, dialogues, autobiography, and reminiscences. He dedicated the section "Poésie brute" to the Argentine writer, editor, and great lady, Victoria Ocampo. See *Œuvres I*, Pléiade (1957), p. 351.

62. *As always it is Caracalla*: Valéry evidently meant to say "Caligula," the Roman emperor who is said to have expressed regret that his people did not have a single neck, by which the entire nation could be decapitated in one blow.

73. MOMENTS: "Instants," a part-title in the volume *Mélange*.

85. BROKEN STORIES: *Histoires brisées* (Gallimard, 1950); see *Œuvres II*, Pléiade (1960), pp. 405–67.

As a frontispiece in the edition of 1950, there is a color drawing of Robinson Crusoe on his island, wearing a plume in his hat. Beneath it are these lines, in Valéry's hand: "Although he was alone on his island, he wore a plume in his hat—it seemed to him that by doing this he created someone to look at the plume."

104. *Gozon*: a character created by Valéry to represent the purely objective observing mind. Like Tiresias, this Gozon is both male and female. To give him credibility, Valéry makes him a descendant of Dieudonné de Gozon, of Provence, a fourteenth-century Grand Master of the Order of St. John of Jerusalem. (See also pp. 111 and 119.)

137. *Maelzel's famous mechanical chess player*: There is a great deal of misinformation surrounding the Maelzel

brothers and the mechanical chess player. It had been invented in 1769, as Poe says in his essay, "Maelzel's Chess-Player," by the Hungarian Baron von Kempelen (1734–1804), and not by one of the Maelzel brothers. Moreover, it was not Leonard Maelzel (1783–1855), inventor of the 42-piece mechanical orchestra called the *panharmonicon*, but rather the older and less famous of the two brothers, Johannes Nepomuk Maelzel (1772–1838), developer of the metronome (1816), who was exhibiting the Von Kempelen chess player in the United States in 1835, when Poe witnessed an exhibition of it in Richmond and wrote his essay. Johannes Maelzel died in 1838 aboard ship, on his way to Philadelphia, where he had intended to settle.

146. *The ox on the...tongue*: "Le bœuf sur la langue"; a proverbial figure meaning "to be silent for some weighty reason," usually with the implication of being paid to keep silent. (βοῦς in Greek means both "money" and "ox.")

151. *Precise and   regulations*: There is no indication in any of the MSS. or the Œuvre (Pléiade) what word Valéry meant in this lacuna. It seems likely, however, on the basis of this short piece's tone, that he may have intended an echo of Descartes' "idées claires et distinctes."

153. ODDS AND ENDS: a group of prose poems selected from the two volumes of Valéry's aphoristic writings, *Tel Quel I* and *II* (Gallimard, 1941 and 1943); see *Œuvres II*, Pléiade (1960), pp. 471–781, *passim*.

The remaining contents, actually the larger part of the *Tel Quel* volumes, appear under the same title, "Odds and Ends," in *Analects*, Vol. 14 of the *Collected Works*.

156. *In eo vivimus et movemur*: "In him we live and move...." *Acts of the Apostles* 17:28.

169. THE TREE: "Arbre." It is unfortunately impossible to translate into English Valéry's onomatopoeic pun in this poem's second line, where by writing "... coup, coup ... ," he suggests both the name and the call of the cuckoo and, indeed, strengthens the metaphor of the tree as a bird.

191. MINIATURES: "Petits textes," first published as *Modes et manières d'aujourd'hui*" (Collection Pierre Carrard, 1923); reprinted under the title "Petits textes," in *N.R.F.*, January 1, 1928.

198. ... *Who dare not take love lightly*: "qui n'osent badiner avec l'amour." Valéry is playing with the title of a comedy by Alfred de Musset, *On ne badine pas avec l'amour* (1834).

205. AGATHA: "Agathe," published first in 1956, on the initiative of Valéry's daughter Agathe Rouart-Valéry. This edition was limited to 190 copies, each composed of a printed text executed by Alberto Tallone and a facsimile of the manuscript by Daniel Jacomet: see *Œuvres II*, (Pléiade 1960), p. 1388. In Valéry's letters to Gide we find an account of the slow, intermittent development of *Agatha*. On January 15, 1898, he wrote:

One morning recently, in my study *sub lumine*, I began writing the following story which I shall never finish because it's too difficult. Given one of those women who sleep two or three or ten years without waking, I assume (quite arbitrarily) that she has dreamed the whole time, and that when she wakes she can recount her dream. Now, for two or three . . . , or ten years, she has had no sensations: therefore, I must study the impoverishment or dwindling (or whatever) of the datum on which she fell asleep. This is a problem in transcendent (or imaginary) psychology, difficult even to conceive. The successive zones of alteration of the images, etc., the variations in thought, as little by little it turns vacant—this would be interesting.

The theme excited me for ten minutes. Then, with no enthusiasm, I wrote a few lines for a start, but having nothing to do with the problem, then stopped. But, typically, I filed away this bit of an opening to study it later on, mathematically—in no way related to literature.

During the next two years (1898–1900), in his letters to Gide, Valéry spoke of *Agatha* twice, briefly, referring to it as "Agatha, or Sleep," and complaining how difficult it was to find the right beginning for it: "But where there's no hitch, there's no pleasure in writing." (August 29, 1900.)

Then on October 17, 1900: "I am considerably bored, writing *Agatha* as a chore—the whole subject has gone cold. I am condemned to write retroactively, with no warmth, no aim, desire, or pleasure—like a perfect imbecile—an imbecile being a man whose job is a crashing bore and who goes on doing it.... I am breaking off this letter ... to give *Agatha* another hour before dinner."

Several months later, Valéry confided a few remarks on *Agatha* to his friend Gustave Fourment (January 12, 1901):

I am writing...something crazy:

My story-to-be, almost the whole of it, is written in the simplest, most abstract language, which will make it seem obscure when it is merely unfamiliar. I have been at it steadily for three months and it's only now taking its first steps—or pages. But just you try introducing *thought* and something *new* into literature; sustained *continuity* in a period of mindless confusion. It's a project so absurd that, in the end, I rather like this deadly stiff bit of writing.

In the notebooks for 1903 (*Cahiers* 3: 106) there is this entry:

The early Agatha—

Here is the plan for Agatha as I conceived it in '98, I think—or '97. A woman falls asleep. I imagine a cataleptic sleep—I mean, indefinitely long. I assume (at some risk) that all sensation is suppressed in her. And I assume, finally, that she does dream and that the succession of images is such that the nth = the 1st. So she is turning in a closed circle, n_1. If we stop at assumptions, that's the end of the matter. If we introduce one new condition—a progressive diminution of her awareness of the cycle, because of the repetition—habit, and the increasing speed of *rotation*—then what? Then perhaps the cycle would be, for her, stabilized—a world governed by a simple, dependable law, an object more and more foreign—which she attempts to *think* about—and so wakes up. Thus: dog, moon, barking, dog, etc. But this rough outline stands for an infinite number of problems, and that is why I drew it.

In 1912, Gide was urging Valéry to put together a collection of his writings for publication by Gallimard, to be composed of: "Your poems, the 'Evening with Teste,' the 'Method of Vinci,' various articles from the *Mercure*, and the fragments of 'Agatha Asleep,' and something else (I forget) that happened in China."

Valéry replied:

I have another idea: to put together a mixed volume—prose, verse—in no order at all, like a notebook made up of works-in-progress, and not presenting oneself as more a poet than anything else.

That way, if time is willing, I can throw together a *Monsieur Teste* like this: 1st "the Soirée"; 2nd the ex-beginning of "Agatha" which would be the *interior* of Teste's night; 3rd a walk with Monsieur Teste (I have the beginning of it), and we could plump out the volume with fragments from my notes.

After all, a book that's all verse is an awful bore. I seem to remember that Nerval put together a mixture of this kind, and for tiny poets it's a mixture that has its advantages.

Valéry seems to have thought only tentatively of "Agathe" as a part of *Monsieur Teste*, and that in view of a publication that never really interested him and never appeared. Rather than agree to Gide's proposal that he put together a makeshift volume, Valéry spent the next five years writing *La Jeune Parque*, published in 1917.

213. PURE DRAMAS: "Purs drames," first published in Francis Viélé-Griffin's little review *Les Entretiens politiques et littéraires*, IV, 24 (March, 1892); see *Œuvres I*, Pléiade (1957), p. 1597.

216. THE OLD ALLEYS: "Les Vieilles Ruelles," dedicated to Huysmans in 1889, but first published in "Paul Valéry et 'À Rebours'," by Henri Mondor, in the *Revue de Paris*, March, 1947; see *Œuvres I*, Pléiade (1957), p. 1599.

Valéry wrote this prose poem at the age of 18, shortly after reading Huysmans' *À Rebours*. A few years before his death in 1945, he gave his original manuscript to Henri Mondor.

218. UNPUBLISHED PAGES: "Pages inédites," first published under the pseudonym André Gill in *Chimère*, No. 4, November, 1891; see *Œuvres I*, Pléiade (1957), p. 1600.

223. ABC: these three poems appeared in Marguerite Caetani's *Commerce V*, Autumn, 1925; the third, poem "C," was republished in Valéry's *Morceaux choisis* (1930).

In the 1920's, Valéry was planning a collection of prose poems to be titled *Alphabet*. The ABC poems were written for that series, which was never completed. In the *Valeryanum* (a collection of Valéry's published works made by Julien P. Monod, and now in the Bibliothèque Jacques Doucet in Paris) there are several prose poems in typescript probably written for *Alphabet*. They are *Attente* "Waiting," *Midi* "Midday," *Le Bain* "The Bath," *Laure* "Laura," *L'Unique* "The Unique," *Accueil du Jour* "Greeting the Day," and *La Rentrée* "The Return." See herein, pp. 229–41 and *nn*.

229. WAITING (SKETCH FOR A POEM): "Attente, Esquisse d'un Poème"; the French text is here published (see below) for the first time.

The typescript of "Attente," in the *Valeryanum* of the Doucet Library, has a note in Julien Monod's hand saying that "Attente" was to be poem "T" in the series *Alphabet*.

Invited to contribute a poem to the "Programme" of the Fifty-fourth Annual Ball of the X (alumni of the École Polytechnique), Valéry offered them "Attente," which was rejected as "too suggestive" (*trop libre*) for the occasion. He then sent them "Midi," which was published in the "Programme." (See "Midday," herein p. 231.)

Attente

Esquisse d'un Poème

...*Tout à coup j'ai le sentiment d'un silence et d'un esprit dans les cheveux de ma nuque. Qui donc est si près de moi que je n'ose tourner la tête et jeter la main pour saisir? Je sais trop que je ferais être ce qui n'existe pas encore.... Je sais bien que je saisirais la chose vivante que vous êtes, et que le changement de toute notre vie est à la portée de ma main. Il est et il n'est pas.... Quelle étrangeté!...*

Tu es là, avec toutes les conséquences ineffables du baiser qui est si proche, et que rien maintenant ne peut plus retenir.

Qu'attends-tu? Tu attends que tu ne puisses plus attendre, et tu sens croître en toi le poids d'une fatalité. Tes lèvres sur mon cou s'abattront comme une pierre....Encore un moment, Monsieur le Bourreau!...

Je regarde et j'entends le balancier de la pendule battre comme le cœur du monde étranger à nos cœurs. Ce temps n'est plus le nôtre. Tout ce qui va venir m'est comme passé. Une chose qui n'est pas encore est tout accompli. Cette chambre contient dans ses murs tous les modes de la durée: ce qui fut, ce qui est, ce qui sera s'échangent dans cette enceinte. Que de pensées inachevées, que de prévisions trop puissantes naissent et meurent dans mon esprit!

Le livre qui est devant moi est illisible; et mon âme, sur ces lignes où mon œil désespérément s'attache sans les voir, attend le choc.

Je me tournerai brusquement vers toi, quand le signal qui est en nous viendra de toi.

231. MIDDAY: "Midi," published in the "Programme" of the Fifty-fourth Annual Ball of the X, March 2, 1937. (See p. 229 and *n*.)

233. THE BATH: "Le Bain," published in *La Revue du Médicin*, April 7, 1930; in Valéry's *Morceaux choisis* (1930).

235. LAURA: "Laure," published in *D'Ariane à Zoé, Alphabet galant et sentimental...*, an album of verse and prose, with lithographs by a number of writers and artists (Librairie de France, 1930); reprinted in *N.R.F.*, January 1, 1931.

237-41. THE UNIQUE: "L'Unique"; GREETING THE DAY: "Accueil du jour"; THE RETURN: "La Rentrée"; these three poems, with a fourth, "Avant toute chose," were published together under the title "Petits Poèmes abstraits" ("Little Abstract Poems") in *La Revue de France*, January 1, 1932. Only "Avant toute chose" was republished in French, as Part I of "Méditation avant pensée," in *Mélange* (1939); see "Meditation Before Thought," herein, p. 61.

Valéry's view of these four poems may be glimpsed in a passage from one of his notebooks (*Cahiers* 15:453): "6 Jan. 32. At the Academy, Bazin drew me aside and to my enormous surprise paid me a great compliment on my 'Abstract Poems' in the *Revue de France*. The mystical tone of these pieces must have made an impression on him. I was amazed. The obscurity of these 'exercises'—with which I am far from satisfied—neither annoyed nor shocked him!..."

243-46. PSALM I: "Psaume"; YOU FORGET: "Tu oublies"; PSALM II: "Psaume"; and [Two Poems]: "Guidé par l'image

...", and "O mes étranges personnages" were published in *Botteghe Oscure*, III and V (Rome), 1949 and 1950.

247. IDEA FOR A STORY: "Idée d'un conte (à la Villiers)," first published in *Mélange de prose et de poésie, Album plus ou moins illustré d'images sur cuivre de l'auteur* (Les Bibliophiles de l'Automobile-Club de France, 1939); withdrawn from the later edition of *Mélange* (Gallimard, 1941); see *Œuvres I*, Pléiade (1957), p. 1716.

This is not the first story by Valéry to be written under the influence of Villiers de l'Isle-Adam.

248. SHORT STORY: a humorous fable, published in the collection *Pensées d'une Amazone* ("Thoughts of an Amazon"), by Natalie Clifford Barney, (Emile-Paul Frères 1921); see *Œuvres II*, Pléiade (1960), p. 1416.

"*Tu penses?...Donc je fuis.*": an obvious allusion, less subtle than most of Valéry's puns, to Descartes' "Je pense, donc je suis," which must nevertheless have amused Natalie Barney, who is something of a *bas-bleu* and has referred to herself, and was so known among her intimate circle of friends, as the "Amazon." The translation is by David Paul.

249. WORK: "Travail," first appeared as "Un poème inédit de Paul Valéry," in *Arts, Spectacles*, No. 399, February 20–26, 1953; with the present title, in *Œuvres I*, Pléiade (1957), p. 1699.

250. REGARDING THE SEA: "Regards sur la mer," first published in *Mer Marines Marins*, Volume I of the collection *Images du Monde*, (Firmin-Didot, 1930); in "Hommage à Mistral," *N.R.F.*, May 1, 1930; in *Pièces sur l'art* (Maurice

Darantière, Epinay-sur-Seine, 1931); see *Œuvres II*, Pléiade (1960), p. 1334.

257. *... what Joseph Vernet called "the various works of a sea-port"*: Vernet was an eighteenth-century French painter from Provence. After twenty years in Rome, painting views of seaports, storms, etc., he was recalled to Paris and by royal command produced a remarkable series of paintings of French seaports, thirty-eight of which are now in the Louvre.

259. HOW TO MAKE A PORT: "Composition d'un port," first published in *Verve*, No. 8 (June 1940); in *Mauvaises Pensées* (1942); see *Œuvres II*, Pléiade (1960), p. 860.

262. POWER OF PERFUMES: "Puissance des Parfums," published in *Parfums*, an album of articles on perfume by Paul Valéry, Jacques de Lacretelle, Louise de Vilmorin, and Colette, with illustrations by Henri Matisse, André Derain, Christian Bérard, and Van Dongen (Raucour, 1945).

265. PARIS IS HERE: "Présence de Paris," written in 1937 and first published in *Regards sur le monde actuel*, Volume J of the collected *Œuvres de Paul Valéry* (N.R.F., 1938); see *Œuvres II*, Pléiade (1960), p. 1011.

*This colophon was chosen from a number of drawings by Paul Valéry of
his favorite device.*

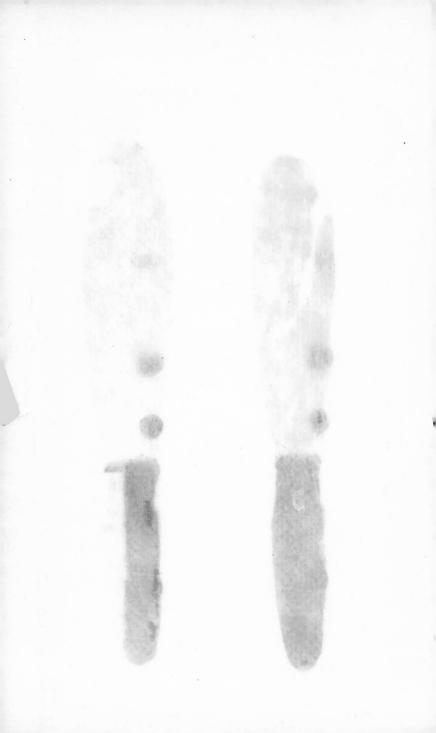